COCKTAILS FROM THE ROAD

POSTMODERN GYPSY

JORDAN POOLE

INTRODUCTION: SHAKEN, STIRRED, AND TRAVELED

Welcome, fellow wanderers and cocktail enthusiasts, to a spirited journey unlike any other. This isn't just another cocktail book—it's a passport to adventure, a roadmap of flavors, and a chronicle of experiences distilled into glass after delicious glass.

Travels across America with a camper named Priscilla
Queen of Backroads

Inspired by the travels and tribulations recounted in "Post Modern Gypsy," this cocktail compendium is a testament to the transformative power of both travel and mixology. Just as our intrepid narrator found enlightenment, friendship, and self-discovery on the open road, we invite you to embark on your own journey of taste and imagination.

Within these pages, you'll find more than just recipes—you'll discover stories. Each cocktail is a chapter, each ingredient a character, and each sip a step further into uncharted territory. From the sun-baked deserts of the American Southwest to the wind-swept plains of the Midwest, from chance encounters with strangers to moments of solitary reflection, we've captured the essence of the nomadic spirit in liquid form.

Piscilla Queen of Backroads(camper) in Mainstreet America

But this book is more than a retelling of one person's adventures. It's an invitation to create your own. We'll teach you the basics of mixology, yes, but we'll also show you how to infuse your creations with the flavors of your own journeys. Whether you're mixing drinks in a fully-stocked home bar or improvising with limited supplies in a camper named Priscilla, we've got you covered.

You'll learn how to craft classics and contemporary cocktails alike, but with a twist that speaks to the heart of the wanderer. We'll explore drinks for every season, non-alcoholic options for when you're the designated driver, and even dive into the art of mobile mixology for those times when the open road calls your name.

So, whether you're a seasoned bartender, a curious novice, or somewhere in between, there's something here for you. This book is for anyone who's ever dreamed of packing up and hitting the road, for those who find poetry in the clinking of ice in a shaker, and for those who believe that the best stories are told over a well-crafted drink.

Grab your shaker, pack your bags, and let's embark on this flavorful journey together. After all, life is a banquet of experiences—and we intend to drink it all in.

looking out down the desert highway from
Priscilla, Queen of Backroads (Camper)

On the Rocks and On the Road: A History of Traveling Cocktails

The story of cocktails and travel is as old as exploration itself. From the grog of sailors to the modern-day camping cocktail kit, the history of mobile mixology is a fascinating journey through time, culture, and ingenuity.

Ancient Roots: The First Travel Drinks

The concept of travel-friendly alcoholic beverages dates back to ancient times. Roman soldiers carried posca, a mix of vinegar, water, and herbs, on their campaigns. Medieval pilgrims often carried ale or wine in flasks, believing alcohol to be safer than water.

The Age of Exploration: Spirits on the High Seas

The real revolution in travel drinks came with the Age of Exploration. Sailors needed drinks that wouldn't spoil on long voyages, leading to the popularity of spirits like rum. The British Navy's daily rum ration, started in 1655, gave birth to many nautical cocktails, including the grog (rum, water, sugar, and lime juice).

The Birth of the Cocktail: A Moveable Feast

The term "cocktail" first appeared in print in 1806, defined as "a stimulating liquor composed of spirits of any kind, sugar, water, and bitters." As Americans pushed westward in the 19th century, saloons became social hubs, and bartenders traveled with settlers, bringing their recipes and techniques to new frontiers.

The Railroad Era: Dining Car Delights

The expansion of railroads in the late 19th century introduced a new era of travel cocktails. Luxury trains like the Orient Express boasted elaborate bar cars where passengers could enjoy professionally mixed drinks while watching the landscape roll by.

Prohibition and Speakeasies: The Portable Party

During Prohibition (1920-1933), the need for discreet, portable drinking solutions led to innovations like the hip flask and the emergence of easily-mixed cocktails that could be quickly dispersed if discovered.

Post-War Boom: The Rise of Leisure Travel

The post-World War II economic boom saw a surge in leisure travel. Tiki culture, born in the 1930s, exploded in popularity, with tropical drinks evoking the spirit of exotic vacations. The first Airstream travel trailer was introduced in 1936, setting the stage for the future of mobile hospitality.

The Jet Age: Mile-High Mixology

As commercial air travel became more common in the 1950s and '60s, airlines competed for customers with luxurious in-flight service, including elaborate cocktail offerings. The glamour of air travel was often embodied in a well-mixed martini served at 30,000 feet.

The Modern Era: From Tailgating to Glamping

The late 20th century saw the rise of new travel-drinking traditions:

1. Tailgating: Originating in the 1920s, tailgate parties became a major part of American sports culture by the 1980s,

with fans mixing drinks in parking lots before games.

2. Festival Culture: Music festivals like Woodstock (1969) and later Burning Man (1986) created new contexts for communal, outdoor drinking experiences.
3. Camping Cocktails: The 21st century has seen a revival of interest in outdoor recreation, coupled with a craft cocktail renaissance. This has led to the development of specialized camping bar tools and portable cocktail kits.
4. Glamping: The "glamorous camping" trend, gaining popularity in the 2010s, has brought high-end cocktail experiences to outdoor settings.

The Digital Age: Social Media and Mobile Mixology

Today, social media has transformed how we share our travel and drinking experiences. Instagrammable cocktails have become a key part of travel culture, with people seeking out unique drinks in picturesque locations.

The Future: Sustainable and Tech-Savvy

As we look to the future, travel cocktail culture is evolving with a focus on sustainability (using local, eco-friendly ingredients) and technology (apps for mobile cocktail recipes, smart shakers, etc.).

From the high seas to the high plains, from dining cars to camper vans, the history of traveling cocktails is a rich tapestry of human ingenuity and the eternal desire to make any journey a little more spirited. As we raise our glasses in our modern-day Priscillas, we're not just enjoying a drink – we're participating in a tradition as old as travel itself.

The Traveling Mixologist's Toolkit: Multi-Purpose Cocktail Equipment

A Coffee Perculator, the perfect Multi-Tasking Container

When you're on the road, space is at a premium. The key to successful mobile mixology is finding equipment that can pull double duty. Here's a guide to assembling a versatile cocktail kit using items you might already have in your travel gear:

1. The Multi-Tasking Mug

Your trusty travel mug isn't just for coffee. A stainless steel insulated mug can serve as:

- A shaker (when paired with another mug or a tight-fitting lid)
- A mixing glass for stirred drinks
- A vessel for hot cocktails

Pro tip: Look for a mug with measurement markings on the inside for easy portioning.

2. The Versatile Coffee Percolator

As demonstrated by our intrepid "Post Modern Gypsy," a coffee percolator is a cocktail-making powerhouse:

- Use the basket as a strainer for shaken or stirred drinks
- The pot itself can serve as a mixing vessel for batch cocktails
- In a pinch, the percolator can be used to heat ingredients for warm cocktails

3. The Indispensable Multi-Tool

A good multi-tool is essential for any traveler, and it's surprisingly useful for cocktail making:

- Use the knife to cut fruit for garnishes
- The can opener works for, well, opening cans
- Some multi-tools even include a corkscrew and bottle opener

4. The Humble Water Bottle

A reusable water bottle can be more than just a vessel for staying hydrated:

- Use it as a shaker for single drinks
- Mix and store batch cocktails for later
- If it has a wide mouth, use it as a muddler for herbs and fruits

5. The Resourceful Reusable Straw

Reusable straws aren't just eco-friendly, they're multi-functional:

- Use as a stirrer for mixed drinks
- A long straw can double as a bar spoon for layered cocktails
- Metal straws can even work as a muddler in a pinch

6. The Clever Collapsible Funnel

A collapsible silicone funnel takes up almost no space but is incredibly useful:

- Strain cocktails if you don't have a dedicated strainer
- Use it to easily pour drinks into narrow-necked bottles
- Handy for adding small amounts of liquids accurately

7. The Indispensable Pocket Knife

A good pocket knife is a bartender's best friend on the road:

- Use it to cut citrus fruits and other garnishes
- Some models include a bottle opener and corkscrew
- Can be used to peel fruits for zests or twists

8. The Trusty Bandana

Don't underestimate the humble bandana:

- Use as a makeshift strainer in emergencies

- Wrap ice in it and crush with a heavy object for crushed ice
- It's perfect for cleaning up spills and wiping down surfaces

9. The Resourceful Resealable Bags

Resealable plastic bags are a traveler's (and mobile bartender's) best friend:

- Use to shake cocktails if you don't have a shaker
- Store pre-made syrups or pre-cut garnishes
- In a real pinch, fill with water and freeze for ice

10. The Ingenious Tea Infuser

A tea infuser isn't just for loose-leaf enthusiasts:

- Use it to infuse spirits with herbs, spices, or fruit
- Works as a small strainer for single drinks
- Can hold spices for mulled wine or cider

Remember, the key to mobile mixology is cre-

ativity and resourcefulness. With these multi-purpose tools in your travel kit, you'll be ready to mix
up delicious cocktails wherever your journey
takes you. As our "Post Modern Gypsy" would
surely agree, the best tool is often the one you already have on hand.

A Glass Growler Jug, perfect for dispensing
any beverage

The Journey of a Post Modern Gypsy: Connecting Travel and Mixology

In the spirit of the "Post Modern Gypsy," the worlds of travel and mixology intertwine like the most intricate of cocktail recipes. Just as our intrepid narrator found enlightenment on the open road, we too can discover the profound connections between journeying and the art of crafting the perfect drink.

The Essence of Discovery

At its core, both travel and mixology are about discovery. When we embark on a journey, we open ourselves to new experiences, cultures, and flavors. Similarly, when we approach the craft of cocktail making, we explore combinations, experiment with ingredients, and push the boundaries of our palate.

Consider the "Desert Mirage" cocktail, born from the high desert experiences of California. It captures the essence of discovery, blending unexpected flavors like prickly pear vodka with the familiar comfort of lime and agave. Each sip is a reminder of the surprises that await us when we venture into the unknown.

Adapting to the Environment

A true Post Modern Gypsy learns to adapt to their environment, making do with what's available and finding beauty in the unexpected. This principle applies equally to the world of mobile mixology.

Remember the ingenious use of a coffee percolator as a cocktail strainer? This embodies the spirit of adaptation. When we travel, we learn to see the potential in everyday objects, transforming them into tools for creating extraordinary experiences. A empty tuna can becomes a makeshift shaker, a flat rock turns into a muddler - the world becomes our bar.

A view from Priscilla's Galley out to the
Arizona desert

Embracing Local Flavors

Every destination has its unique flavors, ingredients, and drinking traditions. The Post Modern Gypsy mixologist embraces these local elements, incorporating them into their craft to create drinks that tell the story of a place.

The "Navajo Sea" cocktail, with its use of blue curaçao to evoke the vast expanse of the desert night sky, exemplifies this approach. It reminds us to look to our surroundings for inspiration, to let the spirit of a place infuse our creations.

The Art of Improvisation

Both the traveler and the mixologist must master the art of improvisation. On the road, plans change, expectations are upended, and we must think on our feet. Behind the bar (or the tailgate), we might find ourselves without a crucial ingredient or tool, forcing us to get creative.

This improvisational spirit gave birth to drinks like the "Fruit Cocktail Dream," born from a moment of intense craving and limited resources. It teaches us that sometimes the most memorable creations come from working with what we have, rather than lamenting what we lack.

Building Connections

Perhaps the most profound similarity between travel and mixology is their power to bring people together. Whether it's sharing a sunset and a cocktail on the roof of Priscilla or mixing up a batch of "Sweet Tea Wanderer" for new friends met on the road, drinks have a way of breaking down barriers and fostering connections.

The Post Modern Gypsy understands that a well-crafted cocktail is more than just a drink - it's a medium for sharing stories, creating memories, and bridging cultural divides.

The Journey Never Ends

Just as the road always beckons with new horizons, the world of mixology is ever-evolving. There are always new techniques to master, flavors to explore, and traditions to discover. The Post Modern Gypsy embraces this never-ending journey, understanding that every destination - whether it's a new town or a new cocktail recipe - is just the beginning of another adventure.

In the end, the Post Modern Gypsy's approach to travel and mixology is about more than just getting from point A to point B, or mixing a drink to quench one's thirst. It's about the journey itself, the stories we collect along the way, and the moments of connection and discovery that turn a simple trip into a life-changing adventure.

So as you flip through these pages, learning about spirits and techniques, remember that each recipe is more than just a list of ingredients - it's an invitation to embark on your own journey of discovery. Whether you're mixing drinks in a fully-stocked home bar or improvising with limited supplies in your own version of Priscilla, you're participating in a grand tradition of exploration, adaptation, and connection.

Now, let's raise a glass to the road ahead, and to the spirits that guide us along the way!

CORE SPIRITS - THE ESSENCE OF LIQUID WANDERLUST

Just as every journey begins with a single step, every great cocktail starts with a foundation of quality spirits. In this chapter, we'll explore the core spirits that form the backbone of mixology - the fuel that powers our liquid travels, if you will.

Think of these spirits as the different modes of transportation in our Post Modern Gypsy adventures. Each has its own character, its own story, and its own way of taking us to new and exciting places:

- Vodka: The versatile companion, ready for any adventure - much like our trusty Priscilla, adapting to whatever the road throws our way.
- Gin: A botanical journey in a glass, reminiscent of those unexpected detours through fragrant, wild landscapes.

- Rum: The spirit of maritime exploration, echoing tales of high seas and distant shores.
- Tequila and Mezcal: Embodying the sun-baked terrains and fiery sunsets of our desert odysseys.
- Whiskey: A time-traveler's drink, each sip a journey through history and tradition.
- Brandy and Cognac: The refined adventurer, bringing Old World elegance to our New World explorations.

As we delve into each of these spirits, we'll not only learn about their production, characteristics, and classic cocktails but also explore how they connect to our travels. We'll discover how each spirit can transport us to different corners of the world, evoking memories of places we've been or inspiring dreams of destinations yet to be explored.

Remember, just as our Post Modern Gypsy found beauty and meaning in unexpected places, we too can find surprising depth and complexity in these familiar spirits. Each bottle is a story waiting to be told, a journey waiting to be taken.

So, fellow travelers and aspiring mixologists,

let's embark on this spirited adventure together. Grab your metaphorical passport (and your very real jigger), and let's explore the world through the lens of these essential elixirs.

As we go, we'll share tips on how to best enjoy these spirits on the road, whether you're mixing drinks on a remote campsite or in the cozy confines of a vintage camper. We'll learn how to make the most of limited resources, how to pair spirits with local ingredients, and how to capture the essence of a place in a glass.

Are you ready to dive into the heart of mixology and emerge with a deeper understanding of both spirits and travel? Then let's begin our journey through the world of core spirits - the first step in mastering the art of liquid wanderlust.

Vodka: The Versatile Companion

Just as our trusty Priscilla adapted to every twist and turn of the open road, vodka stands as the chameleon of the spirit world, ready to take on any flavor profile or mixing challenge we throw its way. This clear, often neutral spirit is the blank canvas of the cocktail world, as versatile and reliable as a well-maintained camper van.

The Spirit of Adaptation

Vodka, like Priscilla, doesn't demand the spotlight. Instead, it provides a sturdy foundation upon which we can build our liquid adventures. Its subtle character allows it to blend seamlessly with a wide array of ingredients, from the fruits found at a roadside stand to the herbs growing wild by your campsite.

Remember how Priscilla transformed from a simple camper to a rolling work of art? Vodka undergoes a similar metamorphosis in our shaker, taking on the personalities of the ingredients we pair it with. It's the ultimate team player in the world of spirits.

The mural on the back of Priscilla, Queen of Backroads

A Global Journeyman

While often associated with Eastern Europe, vodka has become a global citizen, much like our Post Modern Gypsy. It's produced worldwide, from the potato vodkas of Poland to the wheat vodkas of Sweden, the corn vodkas of America to the rice vodkas of Japan. Each variety carries subtle hints of its origins, inviting us to explore the world through our glass.

Practical Portability

One of vodka's greatest strengths for the traveling mixologist is its versatility in storage and transportation. Unlike some spirits that may degrade in heat or light, vodka maintains its integrity in a variety of conditions. This makes it an ideal companion for road trips, camping expeditions, or impromptu tailgate parties.

Vodka Cocktails: Adaptations on the Road

Let's explore a few vodka cocktails that embody the spirit of adaptation and travel:

1. **The Priscilla Sunrise** (Vodka variation)

- 2 oz Vodka
- 3 oz Orange juice
- Splash of grenadine
- Orange slice for garnish

1. Method: Build in a glass over ice, float grenadine on top. Garnish with an orange slice. This variation of our tequila-based Priscilla Sunrise shows how easily vodka can step in when another spirit isn't available. It's a reminder of those moments when we had to improvise on the road, making the best of what we had on hand.

1. **Desert Mirage**

- 2 oz Prickly pear-infused vodka
- 1 oz Lime juice
- 0.5 oz Agave nectar
- Soda water to top
- Dehydrated lime wheel for garnish

1. Method: Shake vodka, lime juice, and agave nectar with ice. Strain into a glass filled with fresh ice, top with soda water. Garnish with a dehydrated lime wheel. This cocktail captures the essence of our desert adventures. The prickly pear infusion can be made by

steeping chopped prickly pear in vodka for 24-48 hours - a perfect project for a multi-day camping trip.

2. **Roadside Stand Smash**

- 2 oz Vodka
- 1 oz Fresh lemon juice
- 0.5 oz Simple syrup
- 3-4 Fresh strawberries (or any seasonal fruit)
- Mint sprig for garnish

1. Method: Muddle strawberries in a shaker. Add vodka, lemon juice, and simple syrup. Shake with ice and strain into a glass filled with crushed ice. Garnish with a mint sprig. This cocktail is an ode to those delightful discoveries at roadside fruit stands. The recipe can be adapted based on whatever local, seasonal fruit you come across in your travels.

Vodka: Your Reliable Co-Pilot

In the end, vodka, like our beloved Priscilla, proves that true character isn't about standing out, but about providing unwavering support for our adventures. It's a reminder that sometimes, the most valuable companions are those that can adapt to any situation, ready to help us make the most of whatever ingredients and experiences the road brings our way.

So the next time you're packing for a journey, consider bringing along a bottle of vodka. Like a trusty Swiss Army knife or a well-worn road atlas, it's a versatile tool that will serve you well, no matter where your travels may lead.

Gin: A Botanical Odyssey

If vodka is the reliable Priscilla of our spirit journey, then gin is the winding, scenic route we couldn't resist taking – a detour into a wild, fragrant landscape that awakens our senses and reminds us why we set out on this adventure in the first place.

The Essence of Exploration

Gin is, at its heart, a spirit of exploration. Its primary flavoring, juniper berries, has been used for centuries for its medicinal properties. But it's the myriad other botanicals – coriander, angelica root, citrus peels, and countless others – that truly make gin a liquid embodiment of a wanderer's spirit.

Each gin is a unique expedition through a botanical wonderland. Like those unexpected detours that led us to breathtaking vistas or hidden meadows bursting with wildflowers, every sip of gin offers a new discovery, a new combination of flavors that tells the story of its origins and creation.

A Global Wanderer with Local Roots

While gin has its roots in the jenever of the Netherlands and the London Dry styles of England, it has become a global wanderer. From the forest-inspired gins of Scandinavia to the citrus-forward gins of Spain, and the native-botanical-infused gins of Australia, each region puts its own stamp on this versatile spirit.

This global gin journey mirrors our own travels in Priscilla. Just as we found unique local cultures and flavors in each new town or landscape, so too does gin absorb and reflect the essence of its birthplace.

The Art of Botanical Balance

Creating a well-balanced gin is much like navigating a complex journey. It requires a delicate balance of flavors, with each botanical playing a crucial role. The juniper provides the backbone – the road that leads us forward. The other botanicals are like the sights, sounds, and smells we encounter along the way, each adding depth and complexity to our journey.

This balance reminds us of those perfect travel days when everything seemed to align – the weather, the scenery, the company, the unexpected discoveries. In a great gin, as in a great journey, all elements work in harmony to create something truly memorable.

Gin Cocktails: Liquid Postcards from Our Travels

Let's explore a few gin cocktails that capture the spirit of botanical exploration and unexpected journeys:

1. **The Forklift Fizz**

- 2 oz Gin
- 1 oz Fresh lemon juice
- 0.5 oz Honey syrup
- Ginger beer to top
- Lemon twist garnish

1. Method: Shake gin, lemon juice, and honey syrup with ice. Strain into a highball glass filled with ice, top with ginger beer. Garnish with a lemon twist. This cocktail, inspired by our adventures with Priscilla, balances the botanical notes of gin with the spicy kick of ginger beer – a reminder that sometimes the most memorable experiences come from unexpected challenges.
2. **Desert Bloom G&T**

- 2 oz Gin
- 4 oz Tonic water
- 2 dashes Orange blossom water
- Edible flower for garnish (desert marigold or prickly pear blossom if available)

1. Method: Build in a glass filled with ice. Stir gently and garnish with an edible flower. A tribute to those moments when we stumbled upon unexpected beauty in the desert. The orange blossom water adds a subtle floral note, reminiscent of desert plants bursting into bloom after a rare rain.
2. **Roadside Herbalist**

- 2 oz Gin
- 0.75 oz Fresh lime juice
- 0.5 oz Simple syrup
- 3-4 Fresh basil leaves
- 2-3 Fresh sage leaves
- Herb sprig for garnish

1. Method: Muddle herbs gently in a shaker. Add gin, lime juice, and simple syrup. Shake with ice and double strain into a chilled coupe glass. Garnish with a fresh herb sprig. This cocktail celebrates those roadside stops where we gathered wild herbs, adding fresh, local flavors to our mobile kitchen. It's a liquid reminder that sometimes the best ingredients are found right outside our door.

Gin: The Spirit of Serendipity

In the end, gin embodies the serendipitous nature of travel. Like those unplanned detours that became the highlights of our journey, gin offers us a chance to explore new flavors, to take the scenic route through a landscape of botanicals.

It reminds us that the joy of the journey often lies not in the destination, but in the unexpected discoveries along the way. Each gin is a new adventure, a new story waiting to be told.

So the next time you're mixing a drink in Priscilla, or around a campfire under the stars, reach for that bottle of gin. Let its complex bouquet of botanicals transport you to wild, fragrant landscapes. Let it remind you of the beauty of the unexpected, and the thrill of exploring the unknown.

Rum: Spirit of Coastal Adventures

If our journey with Priscilla was a cross-country odyssey, rum invites us to drop anchor and savor the flavors of coastal living. This spirit, born in the Caribbean and shaped by centuries of maritime tradition, evokes memories of salty air, sandy beaches, and the gentle rhythm of waves lapping at the shore.

A Personal Voyage

Rum's story resonates deeply with my own journey of coastal living. During my time at the

Savannah College of Art and Design (SCAD), I made my home in a camper at the Rivers End Campground on Tybee Island. Those days of studying by the sea, with the taste of salt in the air and the sound of waves as a constant companion, left an indelible mark on my perception of rum.

Just as rum is infused with the essence of its tropical origins, my experiences on Tybee Island infused my life with the spirit of coastal adventure. The campground became my port, my camper my ship, as I navigated the waters of higher education and artistic discovery.

The Diversity of Island Life

Rum, like the ever-changing moods of the sea, presents a diverse array of styles and flavors. From the light, crisp rums that remind me of sunny days on Tybee's beaches to the rich, full-bodied rums that echo the depth of the Atlantic, each style tells a story.

The variety in rum mirrors the diversity I found in island life. Just as no two days on Tybee were the same, with each tide bringing new treasures to the shore, no two rums are identical. Each offers a unique experience, a new flavor to savor, much like the constantly evolving artworks we created at SCAD.

The Art of Aging and Academic Growth

Many rums gain their complex flavors

through years of aging in oak barrels. This process of maturation parallels my own growth during those university years. Just as my time on Tybee shaped and refined me, transforming me from a freshman to a graduated artist, time transforms rum, developing deep, nuanced flavors.

The patience required for aging fine rum mirrors the dedication needed to complete a degree while living in a camper. It reminds me that sometimes, the best results come to those who are willing to take their time and savor the journey.

Rum Cocktails: Liquid Memories of Coastal Days

Let's explore a few rum cocktails that capture the spirit of coastal living and academic adventure:

1. **Tybee Sunset**

- 2 oz Aged rum
- 1 oz Fresh orange juice
- 0.5 oz Fresh lime juice
- 0.5 oz Grenadine
- Orange half-wheel and cherry for garnish

1. Method: Shake all ingredients except grenadine with ice. Strain into a glass filled with crushed ice. Float grenadine on top. Garnish with orange and cherry. This drink is inspired by the breathtaking sunsets I witnessed from the beaches of Tybee Island, a perfect end to long days of classes and studio work.
2. **SCAD Swizzle**

- 2 oz Light rum
- 1 oz Falernum
- 0.75 oz Lime juice
- 0.5 oz Simple syrup
- 2-3 dashes Angostura bitters
- Mint sprig for garnish

1. Method: Build in a tall glass filled with crushed ice. Swizzle until the outside of the glass frosts. Top with additional crushed ice and garnish with a mint sprig. This refreshing cocktail pays homage to the creative energy of SCAD, with its complex layers of flavors representing the multifaceted nature of an art education.
2. **Campground Daiquiri**

- 2 oz White rum
- 1 oz Fresh lime juice
- 0.75 oz Simple syrup
- Lime wheel for garnish

1. Method: Shake all ingredients with ice. Strain into a chilled coupe glass. Garnish with a lime wheel. A stripped-down, elemental cocktail that reminds me of the simple pleasures of camper life - proving that sometimes, less truly is more.

Rum: The Spirit of Coastal Living

In essence, rum embodies the spirit of coastal adventure that defined my university years. It reminds me of the joy of discovery, the allure of the ocean, and the rich tapestry of experiences that await those bold enough to make their home where the land meets the sea.

Each sip of rum is an invitation to revisit those formative years, to let our imaginations set sail for the shores of Tybee Island. It encourages us to embrace the spirit of exploration, whether we're actually by the sea or simply dreaming of coastal breezes from wherever we may be.

So the next time you pour yourself a glass of rum, take a moment to appreciate the coastal memories in your hand. Let its rich flavors transport you to sun-drenched beaches and bustling seaside campgrounds. And remember, whether in a camper on Tybee Island or in Priscilla on the open road, home is where you park it.

Tequila and Mezcal: Spirits of the Desert

If our journey with Priscilla led us through sun-baked terrains and fiery sunsets, then Tequila and Mezcal are the liquid embodiment of those desert odysseys. These spirits, born from the heart of agave plants under the scorching Mexican sun, capture the essence of arid landscapes and the resilient spirit of desert dwellers.

Children of the Agave

Tequila and Mezcal, though cousins in the agave spirit family, each tell a unique story of the Mexican landscape. Tequila, made specifically from blue agave in designated regions, speaks of cultivated fields and industrial precision. Mezcal, on the other hand, can be made from numerous agave varieties, often wild-harvested, and tells a tale of rugged wilderness and artisanal tradition.

This duality reminds us of our own desert travels - the contrast between well-trodden paths and those remote, untamed stretches where Priscilla's resilience was truly tested.

The Terroir of Tenacity

Like the desert plants that inspired them, Tequila and Mezcal are testament to nature's tenacity. Agave plants, thriving in harsh conditions where other crops would wither, take years to mature - some varieties up to three decades. This slow growth imbues these spirits with a sense of patience and perseverance.

In our travels, we too learned the value of patience and resilience. Those long stretches of desert highway, where mirages danced on the horizon, taught us that sometimes the journey itself is the destination.

The Smoke and Fire of Adventure

While Tequila offers crisp, clean flavors of the agave, Mezcal brings an additional layer of complexity with its characteristic smokiness - a result of roasting agave hearts in underground pits before fermentation and distillation.

This smoky note evokes memories of campfires under starry desert skies, of stories shared and friendships forged in the vast quietude of the wilderness. It's a reminder of the raw, primal connection we feel to the land when we step off the beaten path.

Tequila and Mezcal Cocktails: Liquid Postcards from the Desert

Let's explore a few cocktails that capture the spirit of our desert adventures:

1. **The Priscilla Sunrise**

- 2 oz Blanco Tequila
- 3 oz Fresh orange juice
- 0.5 oz Grenadine
- Orange slice and a cocktail cherry for garnish

1. Method: Build in a glass over ice, slowly pour grenadine down the side of the glass to create a sunrise effect. Garnish with an orange slice and cherry. This

cocktail, our signature drink, mimics the breathtaking sunrises we witnessed over desert horizons. Each sip is a reminder of new beginnings and the promise of adventure that each day brought.

2. **Smoky Desert Night**

- 1.5 oz Mezcal
- 0.75 oz Fresh lime juice
- 0.5 oz Agave nectar
- 2 dashes Orange bitters
- Lime wheel and salt rim for garnish

1. Method: Shake all ingredients with ice. Strain into a rocks glass with a salted rim, filled with fresh ice. Garnish with a lime wheel. This cocktail captures the essence of cool desert nights, with the smokiness of Mezcal evoking memories of evening campfires under vast, star-filled skies.

2. **Prickly Pear Oasis**

- 2 oz Silver Tequila
- 1 oz Prickly pear puree
- 0.75 oz Fresh lime juice
- 0.5 oz Triple sec
- Prickly pear slice for garnish

1. Method: Shake all ingredients with ice. Strain into a coupe glass. Garnish with a prickly pear slice. Inspired by those unexpected splashes of color in the desert - like stumbling upon a blooming cactus - this vibrant cocktail reminds us that beauty can be found in the most unlikely places.

Tequila and Mezcal: Spirits of Exploration

In essence, Tequila and Mezcal embody the spirit of desert exploration that drove some of our most memorable adventures in Priscilla. They remind us of the raw beauty of arid landscapes, the resilience required to thrive in challenging environments, and the rich cultural heritage of the regions they come from.

Each sip of these agave spirits is an invitation to revisit sun-baked highways, towering saguaro cacti, and the profound silence of the desert. They encourage us to embrace the spirit of adventure, to seek out the hidden oases in life, and to appreciate the slow, patient process of growth and transformation.

So the next time you pour yourself a glass of Tequila or Mezcal, take a moment to appreciate the years of patience and the harsh beauty captured in your glass. Let the flavors transport you back to those desert odysseys, to the fiery sunsets and star-filled nights. And remember, like the agave plant itself, sometimes the most remarkable journeys require us to put down roots in unlikely places, to weather storms, and to bloom spectacularly when our moment comes.

Whiskey: A Time Traveler's Tipple

If our journey with Priscilla was a voyage through the physical landscape of America, then whiskey is our ticket to travel through time. Each sip of this amber elixir is a journey through history and tradition, a liquid connection to generations past and a bridge to futures yet unwritten.

The Spirit of Ages

Whiskey, in its myriad forms, is a testament to the ingenuity and craftsmanship of distillers throughout history. From the peated Scotch whiskies that evoke mist-covered Highland moors to the sweet bourbon that speaks of sun-drenched Kentucky cornfields, each style is a time capsule of its origin.

In our travels, we often found ourselves traversing landscapes that seemed frozen in time – small towns where traditions held strong, or historic sites that transported us to another era. Whiskey, like these places, has the power to collapse time, bringing the past vividly into the present.

A Journey Across Continents and Centuries

Just as our road trip took us across the diverse landscapes of America, whiskey takes us on a global voyage:

- Scotch whisky transports us to the rugged coasts and misty glens of Scotland.
- Irish whiskey tells tales of emerald hills and ancient Celtic legends.
- Bourbon and rye whiskey evoke images of America's frontier spirit and Prohibition-era speakeasies.
- Japanese whisky speaks of meticulous craftsmanship and the harmonious blend of tradition and innovation.

Each style is a reflection of its homeland's history, climate, and culture – a liquid geography lesson and history book rolled into one.

The Alchemy of Time

Unlike clear spirits that are ready almost immediately after distillation, whiskey requires patience. It must be aged in wooden barrels, sometimes for decades, to develop its complex flavors. This aging process is a kind of alchemy, where time itself becomes an ingredient.

In our own journey, we learned that some of the most rewarding experiences came from slowing down, from allowing ourselves the time to truly absorb the spirit of a place. Whiskey reminds us of the value of this patience, of the rich rewards that come from giving things the time they need to mature and develop.

Whiskey Cocktails: Liquid Time Machines

Let's explore a few whiskey cocktails that capture the spirit of time travel and tradition:

1. **The Gypsy's Old Fashioned**

- 2 oz Bourbon whiskey
- 1 tsp Sugar
- 2-3 dashes Angostura bitters
- Orange peel for garnish

1. Method: In a rocks glass, muddle sugar with bitters and a splash of water. Add bourbon and ice, stir until well-chilled. Express the oils of an orange peel over the drink and use as garnish. This classic cocktail, with roots stretching back to the early 19th century, is like a liquid time machine. As we sipped these on quiet evenings in Priscilla, we could almost hear the whispers of bygone eras.

2. **Misty Mountain Hop**

- 2 oz Peated Scotch whisky
- 0.75 oz Fresh lemon juice
- 0.5 oz Honey syrup
- 2 dashes Aromatic bitters
- Lemon twist for garnish

1. Method: Shake all ingredients with ice. Strain into a rocks glass filled with fresh ice. Garnish with a lemon twist. Inspired by the foggy peaks we encountered on our journey, this cocktail uses smoky Scotch to evoke misty mountaintops and ancient landscapes.
2. **Prairie Time Flip**

- 2 oz Rye whiskey
- 0.5 oz Maple syrup
- 1 Whole egg
- Nutmeg for garnish

1. Method: Dry shake all ingredients, then shake again with ice. Double strain into a chilled coupe glass. Garnish with freshly grated nutmeg. This rich, creamy cocktail pays homage to the

hearty drinks of America's pioneering days. Sipping it, we could imagine ourselves gathered around a prairie campfire, swapping tales of the day's adventures.

Whiskey: The Spirit of Timeless Adventure

In essence, whiskey embodies the spirit of timeless adventure that drove our journey in Priscilla. It reminds us that while we may be Post Modern Gypsies, we're also part of a long lineage of wanderers and explorers, connected through time by our shared spirit of curiosity and adventure.

Each sip of whiskey is an invitation to time travel, to connect with the history and traditions that have shaped our world. It encourages us to appreciate the passage of time, to respect the wisdom of tradition while embracing the excitement of the new and unexplored.

So the next time you pour yourself a dram of whiskey, take a moment to appreciate the years of history in your glass. Let its complex flavors transport you across time and space, from Scottish Highlands to Kentucky hollers, from Dublin pubs to Tokyo distilleries. And remember, whether you're on the road or reminiscing about past adventures, whiskey is always ready to be your time-traveling companion, helping you bridge the gap between past, present, and future.

Brandy and Cognac: Refined Spirits of Adventure

If our journey with Priscilla was a foray into the wild and untamed landscapes of America, then Brandy and Cognac represent those moments when we sought a touch of refinement amidst our rugged adventures. These spirits, steeped in Old World tradition, bring a sense of elegance and sophistication to our New World explorations.

The Essence of Refinement

Brandy, distilled from wine or fermented fruit juice, and Cognac, a specific type of brandy from the Cognac region of France, are the embodiment of Old World craftsmanship. Their production methods, honed over centuries, speak to a dedication to quality and a respect for tradition that we found echoed in the historic towns and long-established communities we encountered on our journey.

A Tale of Two Worlds

While deeply rooted in European tradition, Brandy and Cognac have found a home in the New World as well. From the Brandy-making traditions of California to the Cognac-inspired American grape brandies, these spirits serve as a bridge between the Old World and the New.

This duality reminded us of our own experiences on the road - how we often found ourselves straddling different worlds, one foot in the familiar and one in the unknown. Like a sip of fine Cognac enjoyed around a campfire, we learned to blend the refined with the rustic, the elegant with the adventurous.

The Art of Patience

Much like whiskey, fine Brandy and Cognac require years of aging to develop their complex flavors. This patience in production taught us to appreciate the slow moments of our journey - those times when we paused to really absorb the beauty of our surroundings, allowing experiences to mature into cherished memories.

Brandy and Cognac Cocktails: Elegance on the Road

Let's explore a few cocktails that capture the spirit of refinement in adventure:

1. **The Gypsy's Sidecar**

   - 2 oz Cognac
   - 1 oz Orange liqueur (such as Cointreau)
   - 0.75 oz Fresh lemon juice
   - Sugar rim and lemon twist for garnish

1. Method: Rim a coupe glass with sugar. Shake all ingredients with ice, strain into the prepared glass. Garnish with a lemon twist. This classic cocktail, enjoyed perhaps after a long day of driving, reminded us that even in the midst of our rustic journey, we could always find a moment of elegance.

2. **Priscilla's Nightcap**

- 1.5 oz Brandy
- 0.5 oz Amaretto
- 2 oz Hot chocolate
- Whipped cream and grated nutmeg for garnish

1. Method: In a mug, combine brandy and amaretto with hot chocolate. Top with whipped cream and a sprinkle of grated nutmeg. On chilly nights when we were huddled in Priscilla, this warm, luxurious drink brought a touch of comfort and sophistication to our mobile home.

2. **Sunset Boulevard**

- 2 oz Cognac
- 0.5 oz Crème de Cassis

- 0.5 oz Fresh lemon juice
- 2 oz Champagne
- Blackberry for garnish

1. Method: Shake Cognac, Crème de Cassis, and lemon juice with ice. Strain into a flute and top with Champagne. Garnish with a blackberry. This effervescent cocktail celebrates those moments when our journey intersected with glamour and excitement, like our unexpected detour to Coachella.

Brandy and Cognac: Elevating the Journey

In essence, Brandy and Cognac embody the spirit of refined adventure that added depth to our journey in Priscilla. They remind us that exploration isn't always about roughing it - sometimes, it's about finding moments of elegance and sophistication in unexpected places.

Each sip of these spirits is an invitation to elevate our experiences, to appreciate the finer things even as we embrace the rugged beauty of the open road. They encourage us to blend the best of the Old World with the excitement of New World discoveries.

So the next time you pour yourself a snifter of Brandy or Cognac, take a moment to appreciate the centuries of tradition in your glass. Let its smooth, complex flavors remind you that refinement can be found anywhere - from the grand boulevards of Paris to a quiet campsite under the stars. And remember, true adventure lies not in choosing between the refined and the rustic, but in learning to appreciate both in equal measure.

LIQUEURS AND FORTIFIED WINES: THE SWEET SYMPHONY OF TRAVEL

As we journeyed across the land in Priscilla, our taste buds embarked on their own adventure. Among the myriad flavors we encountered, liqueurs and fortified wines stood out as the sweet melody in the symphony of our travels. These diverse and often misunderstood spirits added depth, complexity, and a touch of sweetness to our liquid explorations, much like the unexpected moments of joy and connection that peppered our road trip.

THE COLORFUL WORLD OF LIQUEURS

Liqueurs are the storytellers of the spirit world. Each bottle contains not just a sweet, flavored alcoholic beverage, but a narrative of history, culture, and craftsmanship. As we traversed the country, we found that liqueurs often served as liquid souvenirs, encapsulating the essence of the places we visited.

What Exactly is a Liqueur?

At its core, a liqueur is a sweet alcoholic beverage made from a distilled spirit that has been flavored with fruit, cream, herbs, spices, flowers, or nuts, and bottled with added sugar. The alcohol content typically ranges from 15% to 55% ABV, making them versatile components in cocktails or delightful sippers on their own.

A Rainbow of Flavors

The world of liqueurs is as varied as the landscapes we encountered on our journey. Here's a glimpse into some of the categories we explored:

1. **Fruit Liqueurs**: These bright, vibrant spirits reminded us of the orchards and wild berry patches we stumbled upon. Examples include:

   - Chambord (black raspberry)
   - Limoncello (lemon)
   - Cointreau and Grand Marnier (orange)

1. **Herb and Spice Liqueurs**: Like the diverse flora we encountered in national parks, these liqueurs offer complex, often medicinal flavors:

   - Jägermeister (56 herbs and spices)
   - Chartreuse (130 herbs, plants, and flowers)
   - Bénédictine (27 plants and spices)

1. **Cream Liqueurs**: Smooth and indulgent, these were our comfort

drinks on chilly nights in Priscilla:

- Baileys Irish Cream
- RumChata
- Amarula Cream

1. **Nut Liqueurs**: These brought back memories of roadside stands selling local nuts:

- Amaretto (almond)
- Frangelico (hazelnut)
- Nocello (walnut)

1. **Coffee and Chocolate Liqueurs**: Perfect for perking up our evening cocktails:

- Kahlúa
- Tia Maria
- Crème de Cacao

The Art of Making Liqueurs

The process of creating liqueurs is a delicate art, not unlike the balance we strived to maintain in our mobile home. The basic steps include:

1. **Flavoring**: This can be done through maceration (soaking ingredients in the

base spirit), percolation (passing the spirit through the flavoring agents), or distillation with the flavoring agents.

2. **Sweetening**: Sugar or other sweeteners are added to balance the flavors and create the characteristic syrupy texture.
3. **Aging**: Some liqueurs are aged to allow flavors to meld and develop complexity.
4. **Bottling**: Many liqueurs are bottled at proof, meaning no additional water is added after blending.

Liqueurs in Cocktails and Cuisine

Throughout our journey, we found liqueurs to be incredibly versatile. They added depth to our cocktails, brought new dimensions to our campfire coffees, and even found their way into our cooking:

- A splash of amaretto in our morning coffee was a luxurious way to start a day of exploration.
- Limoncello drizzled over fresh berries made for a simple yet elegant dessert under the stars.
- A touch of Chambord in a pan sauce elevated our campsite cooking to

gourmet levels.

FORTIFIED WINES - STRENGTH IN TRADITION

As we ventured into historic towns and spoke with local wine enthusiasts, we gained a new appreciation for fortified wines. These robust, complex beverages served as a bridge between the worlds of wine and spirits, much like how our journey bridged the gap between our past lives and the open road.

Wine casks at Hampton Court Palace

What Makes a Wine Fortified?

Fortified wines are created by adding a distilled spirit, usually brandy, to wine. This process originally served to preserve wine for long sea voyages, but it resulted in a unique category of beverages prized for their rich flavors and higher alcohol content (typically 17-20% ABV).

The Major Players in Fortified Wines
Vermouth

Vermouth became our go-to for adding depth and complexity to cocktails. This aromatized, fortified wine is infused with various botanicals, roots, and herbs.

- **Dry Vermouth**: Light in color and flavor, it's essential in Martinis and other classic cocktails.

- **Sweet Vermouth**: Darker and sweeter, it's a key component in Manhattans and Negronis.

We found vermouth to be incredibly versatile. A splash of dry vermouth in a pan of sautéing mushrooms added an unexpected layer of flavor to our campsite meals.

Port

Port, the rich, sweet wine from Portugal's Douro Valley, became our preferred nightcap during our travels. Its varieties offered a range of experiences:

- **Ruby Port**: Young, fruit-forward, and perfect for mixing in cocktails.
- **Tawny Port**: Aged in wood, with nutty, caramel flavors that paired beautifully with the s'mores we made around the campfire.
- **Vintage Port**: The pinnacle of port production, which we saved for special occasions on our journey.

Sherry

Sherry, hailing from southern Spain, offered us a spectrum of flavors that matched the diversity of landscapes we traversed:

- **Fino**: Dry and crisp, it was our go-to aperitif on warm evenings.
- **Amontillado**: Nutty and complex, it paired wonderfully with the aged cheeses we picked up at local markets.
- **Oloroso**: Rich and full-bodied, it stood up to the heartiest stews we cooked over our camping stove.
- **Pedro Ximénez**: Intensely sweet, it was dessert in a glass, perfect for sipping under the stars.

Madeira

This unique wine from the Portuguese island of Madeira fascinated us with its ability to last for decades, even centuries, after opening. Its styles range from dry to sweet:

- **Sercial**: The driest style, which made for a refreshing aperitif.
- **Verdelho**: Medium-dry, versatile with food pairings.
- **Bual**: Rich and medium-sweet, perfect with desserts.
- **Malmsey**: The sweetest style, a dessert in itself.

The Art of Fortification

The process of creating fortified wines varies depending on the specific type, but generally involves the following steps:

1. **Fermentation**: The base wine is produced through standard fermentation.
2. **Fortification**: A grape spirit is added, which stops fermentation and determines the wine's final sweetness.
3. **Aging**: Many fortified wines undergo extensive aging, developing complex flavors.

The timing of fortification is crucial:

- For sweet wines like Port, spirits are added before fermentation is complete, leaving residual sugar.
- For dry fortified wines, spirits are added after fermentation, resulting in less sweetness.

Fortified Wines in Cocktails and Cuisine
Throughout our journey, we discovered numerous ways to incorporate fortified wines into our mobile lifestyle:

- A splash of dry sherry in our seafood dishes added a touch of sophistication to our beachside meals.
- Port reduction became our secret weapon for elevating simple sauces for grilled meats.
- Madeira found its way into our mushroom risotto, adding depth and complexity.

FEATURE COCKTAIL - "QUILT OF MEMORIES"

As we traveled, we collected memories like patches for a quilt, each one unique yet part of a greater whole. This cocktail, inspired by those patchwork memories, blends the comfort of Southern traditions with the freshness of new experiences.

The Story Behind the Drink

The "Quilt of Memories" cocktail was born on a warm evening in Georgia, as we sat outside Priscilla, sharing stories with locals about their family traditions. The tale of a grandmother's cherished quilt, passed down through generations, each patch holding a story, inspired this drink.

Ingredients:

- 1.5 oz Southern Comfort
- 0.5 oz Peach Schnapps
- 2 oz Cranberry Juice
- 1 oz Orange Juice
- Orange slice and peach slice for garnish

Method:

1. Fill a shaker with ice.
2. Add Southern Comfort, Peach Schnapps, cranberry juice, and orange juice.
3. Shake vigorously for about 10 seconds.
4. Strain into a glass filled with ice.
5. Garnish with an orange slice and a peach slice.

The Flavors Unfolded

Each component of this cocktail represents a piece of our journey:

- **Southern Comfort**: A whiskey-based liqueur that embodies the warmth and hospitality we encountered in the South.

- **Peach Schnapps**: A nod to Georgia's famous peaches and the sweet moments of our travels.
- **Cranberry Juice**: Representing the tart experiences that balanced the sweet, and the vibrant colors of autumn we witnessed.
- **Orange Juice**: Symbolizing the bright, fresh starts each new day on the road brought us.

Variations on a Theme

Just as every family's quilt is unique, this cocktail can be adapted to personal tastes or available ingredients:

- **The Mountain Pass**: Swap cranberry juice for blackberry juice for a deeper, more complex flavor.
- **Desert Sunrise**: Use blood orange juice instead of regular orange juice for a stunning color and slightly different citrus note.
- **Coastal Breeze**: Add a splash of coconut rum to evoke memories of beachside relaxation.

The Tapestry of Tastes

As we reflect on our journey through the world of liqueurs and fortified wines, we're struck by how these diverse beverages mirror the patchwork of experiences that made up our travels in Priscilla. Each sip, like each mile of road, offered something new to discover.

Liqueurs taught us about the power of sweetness to enhance and transform, much like how the kindness of strangers often sweetened our journey. Fortified wines showed us that strength can come from unexpected places, reminding us of the resilience we found within ourselves on the open road.

And our "Quilt of Memories" cocktail? It

stands as a liquid embodiment of our adventure - a blend of traditions and new experiences, of comfort and excitement, of the familiar and the unknown. It reminds us that the best journeys, like the best drinks, are often a carefully balanced mix of diverse elements.

As you explore these spirits in your own mixing and sipping, we encourage you to approach them with the same sense of adventure and openness that guided our travels. Let each taste transport you to new places, evoke cherished memories, and perhaps inspire your own journeys, whether on the road or in the realm of flavors.

After all, isn't that what the spirit of a Post Modern Gypsy is all about? Cherishing traditions while embracing new experiences, finding the extraordinary in the everyday, and always, always being ready for the next adventure - be it in a glass or on the open road.

CLASSIC COCKTAILS: TIMELESS ELIXIRS OF ADVENTURE

As we traversed the country in our trusty Priscilla, we found that classic cocktails were like old friends - familiar, comforting, yet always ready to surprise us with new facets of their personality. These timeless drinks became our liquid companions, each sip a testament to the enduring power of well-crafted simplicity. Just as the open road connected us to the timeless spirit of adventure, these classic cocktails connected us to the rich history of mixology.

TIMELESS RECIPES

Let's dive into some of the most iconic classic cocktails, each with its own story and a special place in our journey.

A martini is shaken and stirred using a Coffee Perculator

1. The Martini: Elegance in a Glass
The Martini is perhaps the most iconic of all

cocktails, a symbol of sophistication that we often turned to when we wanted to add a touch of glamour to our rustic travels.

Recipe:

- 2.5 oz Gin (or vodka for a Vodka Martini)
- 0.5 oz Dry Vermouth
- Garnish: Olive or lemon twist

Method: Stir ingredients with ice in a mixing glass. Strain into a chilled martini glass. Garnish with an olive or a lemon twist.

Travel Tale: We mixed Martinis on a starry night in the desert, the clean, crisp flavors a stark contrast to our rugged surroundings. It reminded us that elegance can be found anywhere - even in the middle of nowhere.

2. Old Fashioned: A Taste of History

The Old Fashioned is a cocktail that truly lives up to its name, with roots stretching back to the early 19th century. It became our go-to drink when we wanted to connect with the historical essence of the places we visited.

Recipe:

- 2 oz Bourbon or Rye Whiskey
- 1 tsp Sugar

- 2-3 dashes Angostura bitters
- Orange peel
- Optional: Cocktail cherry for garnish

Method: In an old-fashioned glass, muddle the sugar with a few drops of water and the bitters. Add whiskey and ice, stir. Express the oils of an orange peel over the drink and drop it in. Optionally, garnish with a cocktail cherry.

Travel Tale: Sipping an Old Fashioned in a small town bar in Kentucky, we felt connected to generations of whiskey lovers before us. The drink's simplicity belied its complexity, much like the seemingly simple life in small-town America.

3. Margarita: The Taste of Sunshine

The Margarita became our liquid sunshine, a refreshing respite that transported us to warmer climes even on the chilliest nights in Priscilla.

Recipe:

- 2 oz Tequila
- 1 oz Fresh lime juice
- 0.5 oz Triple sec or Cointreau
- Salt for rimming (optional)
- Lime wheel for garnish

Method: If desired, rim a rocks glass with salt. Shake all ingredients with ice, strain into the prepared glass filled with fresh ice. Garnish with a lime wheel.

Travel Tale: We mixed Margaritas on a beach in California, the salt on the rim mirroring the salt in the air. It was a moment of perfect harmony between drink and environment.

4. Manhattan: Urban Sophistication

The Manhattan brought a touch of city sophistication to our rural wanderings, a reminder of the urban jungles we'd left behind but occasionally longed for.

Recipe:

- 2 oz Rye Whiskey or Bourbon
- 1 oz Sweet Vermouth
- 2-3 dashes Angostura bitters
- Cocktail cherry for garnish

Method: Stir ingredients with ice in a mixing glass. Strain into a chilled coupe glass. Garnish with a cocktail cherry.

Travel Tale: We enjoyed Manhattans at a jazz club in New Orleans, the drink's complex flavors a perfect match for the intricate melodies swirling around us.

5. Negroni: A Bitter Beauty

The Negroni, with its perfect balance of bitter and sweet, became our preferred aperitif, awakening our palates for the culinary adventures ahead.

Recipe:

- 1 oz Gin
- 1 oz Campari
- 1 oz Sweet Vermouth
- Orange slice for garnish

Method: Stir all ingredients with ice in a mixing glass. Strain into an ice-filled rocks glass. Garnish with an orange slice.

Travel Tale: We discovered the joy of the Negroni in a small Italian restaurant in San Francisco, its bitter complexity a perfect prelude to a hearty pasta dinner.

6. Daiquiri: Simplicity Perfected

The Daiquiri, often misunderstood and over-complicated, showed us the beauty of simplicity - a lesson that served us well on our minimalist journey.

Recipe:

- 2 oz White Rum
- 1 oz Fresh lime juice
- 0.5 oz Simple syrup
- Lime wheel for garnish

Method: Shake all ingredients with ice. Strain into a chilled coupe glass. Garnish with a lime wheel.

Travel Tale: We mixed Daiquiris on a hot afternoon in Florida, the drink's bright, clean flavors cutting through the humidity like a refreshing breeze.

7. Moscow Mule: A Copper-Clad Classic

The Moscow Mule, with its signature copper mug, taught us that sometimes the vessel is as important as what's inside it - a metaphor for how Priscilla herself enhanced our travel experiences.

Recipe:

- 2 oz Vodka
- 0.5 oz Fresh lime juice
- Ginger beer to top
- Lime wedge for garnish

Method: Fill a copper mug with ice. Add vodka and lime juice, top with ginger beer. Stir gently and garnish with a lime wedge.

Travel Tale: We enjoyed Moscow Mules at a roadside diner in the Midwest, the spicy kick of ginger beer complementing the hearty local cuisine.

8. Whiskey Sour: Tart and Timeless

The Whiskey Sour became our go-to drink for

those moments when we needed a pick-me-up, its bright flavors a perfect antidote to the occasional monotony of long drives.

Recipe:

- 2 oz Bourbon
- 1 oz Fresh lemon juice
- 0.5 oz Simple syrup
- Optional: 0.5 oz Egg white
- Cocktail cherry and lemon wheel for garnish

Method: If using egg white, dry shake all ingredients first. Then shake all ingredients with ice. Strain into a rocks glass filled with ice. Garnish with a cocktail cherry and lemon wheel.

Travel Tale: We mixed Whiskey Sours in Priscilla during a rainstorm in the Pacific Northwest, the drink's sunny flavors a stark contrast to the gray skies outside.

9. Mojito: A Refreshing Respite

The Mojito, with its fresh mint and lime, became our liquid air conditioning on hot summer days, a refreshing respite from the heat of the road.

Recipe:

- 2 oz White Rum

- 1 oz Fresh lime juice
- 0.5 oz Simple syrup
- 6-8 Mint leaves
- Soda water to top
- Mint sprig for garnish

Method: In a highball glass, muddle mint leaves with simple syrup and lime juice. Add rum and fill the glass with ice. Top with soda water, stir gently, and garnish with a mint sprig.

Travel Tale: We enjoyed Mojitos at a Cuban-inspired food truck in Miami, the drink's refreshing flavors a perfect match for the vibrant street food.

10. Sazerac: A New Orleans Classic

The Sazerac, with its unique preparation and potent flavors, became our ritual drink, a moment of mindfulness in the midst of our whirlwind journey.

Recipe:

- 2 oz Rye Whiskey
- 0.5 oz Simple syrup
- 2-3 dashes Peychaud's bitters
- Absinthe rinse
- Lemon peel for garnish

Method: Rinse a chilled old-fashioned glass

with absinthe and discard excess. In a mixing glass, stir rye, simple syrup, and bitters with ice. Strain into the prepared glass. Express the oils of a lemon peel over the drink and discard the peel.

Travel Tale: We savored Sazeracs in the French Quarter of New Orleans, feeling connected to the city's rich cocktail history with every sip.

HOW CLASSIC COCKTAILS INSPIRE MODERN TRAVELS

As we journeyed across the country, we found that classic cocktails were more than just drinks - they were gateways to history, culture, and new experiences. Here's how these timeless elixirs inspired our modern travels:

1. Connecting with Local History

Many classic cocktails have strong ties to specific locations. By seeking out these drinks in their places of origin, we connected more deeply with local history and culture.

For instance, our quest for the perfect Sazerac led us to explore the rich cocktail history of New Orleans. We visited historic bars, learned about the city's unique drinking culture, and even took a cocktail tour that illuminated the broader history of the Big Easy.

2. Seeking Out Craft Distilleries

Our appreciation for classic cocktails inspired us to seek out craft distilleries across the country. We discovered that many small-batch producers are creating spirits specifically designed to elevate classic cocktails.

In Kentucky, our love for the Old Fashioned led us to explore bourbon distilleries, both large and small. We learned about the distilling process, the importance of limestone-filtered water, and how different mash bills affect the final product.

3. Exploring Local Ingredients

Local market in France with local ingredients

Classic cocktails often showcase local ingredients, inspiring us to explore farmers' markets and roadside stands in search of the freshest produce for our drinks.

Our passion for Mojitos, for example, led us to grow our own mint in a small herb garden in Priscilla. We'd pick up local honey or agave nectar to use in place of simple syrup, giving our drinks a unique taste of each region we visited.

4. Connecting with Locals

Talking about classic cocktails proved to be an excellent way to connect with locals wherever we went. Bartenders, in particular, were always eager to share their own twists on classic recipes or recommend local spirits.

In a small town in Wisconsin, a conversation about the Brandy Old Fashioned (a local variation) led to an invitation to a backyard barbecue, where we made new friends and learned about local traditions.

5. Inspiring Detours

Sometimes, our cocktail quest led us off the beaten path. We'd hear about a bar famous for its Martinis or a distillery crafting an exceptional gin, and suddenly our route would change to accommodate this new adventure.

These detours often led to some of our most memorable experiences, proving that sometimes the best journeys are the unplanned ones.

6. Enhancing Culinary Experiences

Our knowledge of classic cocktails enhanced our overall culinary experiences on the road. We learned to pair drinks with local cuisines, creating memorable dining experiences.

For instance, we discovered that a well-made Margarita pairs beautifully with spicy South-western cuisine, while a Negroni is the perfect aperitif before a hearty Italian meal.

7. Crafting Our Own Travel Traditions

Inspired by the rituals surrounding classic cocktails, we began to create our own travel traditions. Every time we crossed a state line, we'd mix a cocktail that we felt represented our destination.

This ritual became a way to mark transitions in our journey and to mindfully engage with each new place we visited.

8. Learning New Skills

Our interest in classic cocktails inspired us to learn new skills. We took a bartending class in

Chicago, learned about foraging for cocktail ingredients in the Pacific Northwest, and even tried our hand at making bitters in a workshop in Portland.

These experiences not only enhanced our cocktail game but also gave us new ways to interact with and appreciate our environment.

9. Appreciating Craftsmanship

Classic cocktails taught us to appreciate craftsmanship in all its forms. From the skill of a bartender executing a perfect throw to mix a Bamboo, to the craftsmanship evident in a well-designed bar tool, we learned to recognize and value expertise and attention to detail.

This appreciation extended to other areas of our travel, from admiring architectural details in the cities we visited to appreciating the skill of artisans we met along the way.

10. Embracing Slow Travel

Finally, classic cocktails inspired us to embrace the concept of slow travel. Just as these drinks require time and care to prepare properly, we learned to slow down and savor our experiences on the road.

We'd take the time to perfect our Martini technique in the evenings, or spend an afternoon learning about the history of the Gimlet. These moments of pause enriched our journey, reminding us that travel is about more than just reaching a destination - it's about savoring the journey itself.

Conclusion: The Timeless Spirit of Adventure

As we reflect on our journey through the landscape of classic cocktails, we're struck by how these timeless drinks mirror the spirit of adventure that drove our travels in Priscilla. Each classic cocktail, like each mile of road, offered something new to discover, even within its familiar framework.

These drinks taught us about the power of tradition and the joy of innovation. They showed us that sometimes, the most extraordinary experiences come from the simplest ingredients, combined with care and respect for craft. They connected us to history while inspiring us to create our own stories.

Most importantly, classic cocktails reminded us that the best journeys, like the best drinks, are often about finding the perfect balance - between bitter and sweet, strong and subtle, familiar and unknown.

As you embark on your own adventures, whether on the road or at your home bar, we encourage you to approach these classic cocktails with the same sense of curiosity and openness that guided our travels. Let each sip transport you to new places, evoke cherished memories, and perhaps inspire your own journeys.

After all, isn't that what the spirit of a Post Modern Gypsy is all about? Honoring traditions while embracing new experiences, finding the extraordinary in the everyday, and always, always being ready for the next adventure - be it in a glass or on the open road.

CONTEMPORARY COCKTAILS: THE NEW FRONTIER OF LIQUID ADVENTURES

As we traversed the country in our trusty Priscilla, we discovered that the world of cocktails, much like the landscape of America, is constantly evolving. While classic cocktails connected us to the past, contemporary cocktails propelled us into the future, showcasing the innovative spirit of modern mixology. These cutting-edge creations became the liquid embodiment of our journey - bold, unexpected, and full of discovery.

Priscilla

MODERN CREATIONS AND VARIATIONS

The contemporary cocktail scene is a vibrant tapestry of creativity, blending new techniques, unexpected ingredients, and reimagined classics. Let's explore some of the trends and techniques that define modern mixology, illustrated by cocktails we encountered (and created) on our journey.

1. Molecular Mixology: The Science of Sipping

Just as our journey pushed the boundaries of traditional travel, molecular mixology pushes the boundaries of traditional bartending. This technique applies scientific principles to cocktail creation, resulting in drinks that are as much about texture and presentation as they are about flavor.

Example: The Smoky Mirror

- 2 oz Mezcal
- 0.75 oz Fresh lime juice
- 0.5 oz Agave syrup
- 1 Egg white
- Angostura bitters for garnish

Method: Dry shake all ingredients, then shake again with ice. Strain into a coupe glass. Use a stencil to create a design on top of the foam with Angostura bitters.

We encountered this drink at a cutting-edge bar in San Francisco. The bartender used a small blowtorch to caramelize the bitters design, creating a smoky aroma that enhanced the mezcal's flavors. It was a multi-sensory experience that reminded us of campfires under starry desert skies.

2. Farm-to-Glass: Embracing Locality

The farm-to-table movement has extended to the bar, with mixologists crafting cocktails using hyper-local, seasonal ingredients. This trend resonated with our own journey, as we often found ourselves incorporating local flavors into our mobile cocktail experiments.

Example: The Forager's Fizz

- 2 oz Gin
- 1 oz Fresh lemon juice
- 0.75 oz Homemade blackberry-thyme syrup
- Soda water
- Fresh blackberries and thyme sprig for garnish

Method: Shake gin, lemon juice, and syrup with ice. Strain into a highball glass filled with ice, top with soda water. Garnish with blackberries and a thyme sprig.

We crafted this drink after a day of foraging in the Pacific Northwest. The blackberry-thyme syrup was made from berries we picked ourselves and thyme growing wild by our campsite. It was a true taste of place, capturing the essence of the lush forests we explored.

3. Sustainability in Mixology: Reducing Waste, Increasing Flavor

As our journey made us more aware of our environmental impact, we were impressed by bars and mixologists committed to sustainable practices. This trend focuses on using every part of an ingredient, reducing waste, and creating unique flavors in the process.

Example: The Whole Citrus

- 2 oz White rum
- 1 oz Whole lemon oleo-saccharum*
- 0.5 oz Campari
- Dehydrated citrus wheel for garnish

*Whole lemon oleo-saccharum: Muddle the peel, flesh, and juice of one lemon with 1/4 cup sugar. Let sit for 2 hours, then strain.

Method: Stir all ingredients with ice. Strain into a rocks glass over a large ice cube. Garnish with a dehydrated citrus wheel.

We learned to make this zero-waste cocktail at a sustainable bar in Portland. It opened our eyes to how we could reduce waste in our own mobile bar, leading us to start dehydrating leftover citrus fruits for future use.

4. Reimagined Classics: Old Favorites, New Twists

Many contemporary cocktails take beloved classics and give them a modern spin. This trend resonated with our own journey, as we often found ourselves reimagining our experiences through new lenses.

Example: The Smoked Maple Old Fashioned

- 2 oz Bourbon
- 0.25 oz Maple syrup
- 2 dashes Orange bitters
- 1 dash Chocolate bitters
- Smoked cinnamon stick for garnish

Method: In a mixing glass, stir bourbon, maple syrup, and bitters with ice. Strain into a rocks glass over a large ice cube. Light one end of a cinnamon stick until it smokes, then place it on the rim of the glass.

We created this variation on a cold night in Vermont, inspired by the surrounding maple forests and the comforting aroma of woodsmoke from nearby cabins. It became our go-to drink for chilly evenings in Priscilla.

5. Global Fusion: A World of Flavors

Just as our journey exposed us to diverse cultures within America, contemporary cocktails often blend flavors and techniques from around the world, creating unique fusion drinks.

Example: The Tokyo Southside

- 2 oz Japanese gin
- 1 oz Fresh lime juice
- 0.75 oz Matcha syrup
- 6-8 Mint leaves
- Shiso leaf for garnish

Method: Muddle mint leaves with matcha syrup in a shaker. Add gin and lime juice, shake with ice. Double strain into a coupe glass. Garnish with a shiso leaf.

We discovered this East-meets-West cocktail at a fusion bar in Seattle. It inspired us to experiment with combining flavors from different culinary traditions in our own cocktail creations.

6. Non-Alcoholic Craft Cocktails: Elevating the Mocktail

As designated drivers for each other on long stretches of road, we came to appreciate the rise of sophisticated non-alcoholic cocktails. This trend treats alcohol-free drinks with the same care and creativity as their spirited counterparts.

Example: The Desert Bloom

- 2 oz Seedlip Spice 94
- 1 oz Fresh grapefruit juice
- 0.5 oz Rosemary-infused honey syrup
- Soda water

- Grapefruit twist and rosemary sprig for garnish

Method: Shake Seedlip, grapefruit juice, and honey syrup with ice. Strain into a highball glass filled with ice, top with soda water. Garnish with a grapefruit twist and rosemary sprig.

This refreshing non-alcoholic cocktail became our daytime drink of choice while exploring the Southwest. It proved that a drink doesn't need alcohol to be complex and satisfying.

7. Tea-Infused Cocktails: Steeping in Flavor

The use of tea in cocktails adds depth, complexity, and sometimes a caffeinated kick. This trend appealed to our love of multi-functional ingredients that could serve us from morning to night.

Example: The Earl Grey MarTEAni

- 2 oz Earl Grey-infused gin*
- 0.75 oz Fresh lemon juice
- 0.5 oz Honey syrup
- Lemon twist for garnish

*Earl Grey-infused gin: Steep 2 tablespoons loose Earl Grey tea in 1 cup gin for 2 hours, then strain.

Method: Shake all ingredients with ice. Strain

into a chilled coupe glass. Garnish with a lemon twist.

We perfected this recipe during a rainy week in the Pacific Northwest. The tea-infused gin became a staple in our mobile bar, versatile enough for both morning pick-me-ups and evening cocktails.

8. Savory Cocktails: Beyond Sweet and Sour

Moving beyond traditionally sweet-focused drinks, savory cocktails incorporate elements more commonly found in cuisine. This trend expanded our perception of what a cocktail could be.

Example: The Umami Mary

- 2 oz Vodka
- 4 oz Tomato juice
- 0.5 oz Lemon juice
- 2 dashes Worcestershire sauce
- 2 dashes Soy sauce
- 1 pinch Wasabi powder
- Nori-wrapped cucumber for garnish

Method: Roll all ingredients with ice between two shaker tins. Strain into a highball glass filled with ice. Garnish with a nori-wrapped cucumber slice.

This umami-rich variation on a Bloody Mary

became our favorite brunch cocktail. We'd often customize it with locally-sourced hot sauces from the places we visited.

THE POST MODERN GYPSY COLLECTION

Inspired by our travels and the innovative spirit of contemporary mixology, we created our own collection of cocktails. Each drink in the Post Modern Gypsy Collection captures a specific moment or feeling from our journey, blending modern techniques with flavors that evoke a sense of place.

1. Desert Mirage

This cocktail was born from the shimmering heat of the Southwestern deserts, where the horizon seemed to dance with illusory lakes and oases.

Ingredients:

- 2 oz Prickly pear vodka
- 1 oz Fresh lime juice
- 0.75 oz Agave nectar
- Soda water
- Dehydrated lime wheel for garnish

Method: Shake vodka, lime juice, and agave nectar with ice. Strain into a collins glass filled with ice. Top with soda water. Garnish with a dehydrated lime wheel.

The Story: We crafted this drink after a long day of driving through the Sonoran Desert. The prickly pear vodka, infused with the fruit of desert cacti, captures the essence of the arid landscape. The lime and agave provide a tart sweetness reminiscent of the unexpected bursts of life we encountered in the desert, while the soda water mimics the shimmering mirages that danced on the distant horizon. The dehydrated lime wheel garnish not only adds a visually striking element but also represents the harsh, moisture-sapping environment of the desert.

Variation - The Mirage Mocktail: Replace the prickly pear vodka with prickly pear juice and a dash of non-alcoholic bitters for a refreshing, alcohol-free version that still captures the essence of the desert.

2. Midnight Madness

This indulgent nightcap was inspired by those long nights of driving, when the lines on the road seemed to blur and the only thing keeping us awake was the promise of adventure (and a good dose of caffeine).

Ingredients:

- 1.5 oz Cold brew coffee liqueur
- 1 oz Vanilla vodka
- 1 oz Heavy cream
- Chocolate-covered espresso beans for garnish

Method: Shake all ingredients with ice. Strain into a chilled coupe glass. Garnish with chocolate-covered espresso beans.

The Story: We concocted this drink during a late-night drive through the Midwest, where endless fields of corn and soy were our only companions. The cold brew coffee liqueur represents the necessary fuel for our journey, while the vanilla vodka adds a touch of sweetness and warmth, like the unexpected kindness of strangers we met along the way. The heavy cream smooths out the edges, just as our travels helped smooth out our rough edges. The chocolate-covered espresso beans garnish adds a playful touch and an extra kick of caffeine.

Variation - The Morning After: For a breakfast-appropriate version, blend the ingredients with ice to create a boozy smoothie, perfect for those mornings when you need a little hair of the dog.

3. The Navajo Sea

This striking blue cocktail pays homage to the vast, star-filled skies we encountered in the Southwest, particularly in Navajo Nation, where the night sky seemed to stretch endlessly like a celestial sea.

Ingredients:

- 1.5 oz Silver tequila
- 0.5 oz Blue curaçao
- 1 oz Fresh lime juice
- 0.75 oz Agave syrup
- Star anise for garnish

Method: Shake all ingredients with ice. Strain into a rocks glass filled with crushed ice. Garnish with a star anise.

The Story: We were inspired to create this cocktail after a night spent stargazing in Canyon de Chelly. The silver tequila represents the clarity of the desert air, while the blue curaçao mimics the deep blue of the night sky. The lime and agave balance the drink with sour and sweet notes, much like how the harsh beauty of the desert is balanced by moments of surprising gentleness. The star anise garnish not only echoes the star-filled sky but also adds an aromatic element that enhances the drinking experience.

Variation - The Milky Way: Float a layer of cream on top of the drink to represent the Milky Way stretching across the night sky. This variation adds a silky texture and a visual element that makes the drink even more evocative of a star-filled night.

4. Route 66 Fizz

While not originally part of our core collection, this cocktail became a favorite as we traveled along stretches of the historic Route 66, embodying the spirit of classic American road trips with a modern twist.

Ingredients:

- 1.5 oz Bourbon
- 0.5 oz Peach liqueur
- 0.75 oz Fresh lemon juice
- 0.5 oz Simple syrup
- 1 Egg white
- Aromatic bitters for garnish

Method: Dry shake all ingredients, then shake

again with ice. Strain into a highball glass without ice. Top with a splash of soda water. Garnish with a few drops of aromatic bitters.

The Story: This drink combines the classic American spirit of bourbon with peach liqueur, evoking the orchards we passed on our journey. The egg white creates a silky texture and a foamy top that resembles the clouds we drove under, while the aromatic bitters on top represent the long, straight roads stretching to the horizon. The combination of flavors - sweet, sour, and bitter - mirrors the range of experiences we encountered on the "Mother Road."

Variation - The Vegan 66: Replace the egg white with aquafaba (the liquid from a can of chickpeas) for a vegan-friendly version that maintains the silky texture and foamy top.

The Ever-Evolving Spirit of Adventure

As we reflect on our journey through the landscape of contemporary cocktails, we're struck by how these innovative drinks mirror the spirit of modern adventure that drove our travels in Priscilla. Each contemporary cocktail, like each new experience on the road, offered something unexpected and exciting.

These drinks taught us about the power of innovation and the joy of experimentation. They showed us that sometimes, the most extraordinary experiences come from combining familiar elements in new and surprising ways. They connected us to the present moment while inspiring us to imagine future possibilities.

Most importantly, contemporary cocktails reminded us that the best journeys, like the best drinks, are often about embracing the unknown, taking risks, and being open to whatever comes next.

As you embark on your own adventures, whether on the road or at your home bar, we encourage you to approach these contemporary cocktails with the same sense of curiosity and openness that guided our travels. Let each sip challenge your preconceptions, awaken your senses, and perhaps inspire your own creations.

After all, isn't that what the spirit of a Post Modern Gypsy is all about? Honoring the past while embracing the future, finding the extraordinary in the everyday, and always, always being ready for the next adventure - be it in a glass or on the open road.

SEASONAL COCKTAILS: SIPPING THROUGH THE CHANGING LANDSCAPE

As we traversed the country in our trusty Priscilla, we found that our cocktail preferences shifted with the changing seasons, much like the landscape around us. The light, refreshing drinks that quenched our thirst under the summer sun gave way to warming, spiced concoctions that kept us cozy during chilly autumn nights. This section explores the art of seasonal cocktail crafting, showcasing how we adapted our mobile bar to the rhythm of nature's calendar.

SPRING/SUMMER DRINKS - REFRESHMENT IN A GLASS

When the days grow longer and the temperatures rise, cocktails tend to become lighter, brighter, and more refreshing. Our spring and summer libations were all about capturing the essence of sun-soaked days and balmy nights.

Key Characteristics of Spring/Summer Cocktails:

1. **Light Base Spirits**: Vodka, gin, light rum, and blanco tequila take center stage.
2. **Fresh Fruits and Herbs**: Berries, citrus, melons, and herbs like mint and basil add vibrant flavors.

3. **Effervescence**: Sparkling wine, soda water, or tonic add a refreshing fizz.
4. **Lower Alcohol Content**: Session cocktails and spritzes allow for leisurely sipping.
5. **Bright Colors**: Visually appealing drinks that mirror the vivid hues of the season.

Essential Techniques for Spring/Summer Cocktails:

1. **Muddling**: To extract flavors from fresh fruits and herbs.
2. **Shaking**: For thorough mixing and proper dilution of juice-heavy drinks.
3. **Building**: Layering ingredients in the glass for visually striking results.
4. **Blending**: For frozen cocktails that beat the heat.

Featured Cocktail: Coachella Sunset

This cocktail encapsulates the spirit of our unexpected detour to the Coachella music festival - vibrant, refreshing, and full of youthful energy.

Ingredients:

- 2 oz Watermelon vodka

- 1 oz Fresh lime juice
- 0.5 oz Simple syrup
- Soda water
- Watermelon wedge for garnish

Method: Shake vodka, lime juice, and simple syrup with ice. Strain into a highball glass filled with fresh ice. Top with soda water. Garnish with a watermelon wedge.

The Story: As we found ourselves swept up in the excitement of Coachella, the need for a refreshing, easy-to-drink cocktail became apparent. The watermelon vodka captured the essence of summer freshness, while the lime added a tart kick that kept us coming back for more. The soda water lengthened the drink, making it perfect for sipping throughout the long, music-filled days. The resulting cocktail was as colorful and vibrant as the festival itself, with a taste that reminded us of lazy summer afternoons and the joy of unexpected adventures.

More Spring/Summer Cocktails from Our Travels:

1. **The Highway Spritz**

- 1.5 oz Aperol
- 3 oz Prosecco

- 1 oz Soda water
- Orange slice for garnish

1. *Method:* Build in a wine glass filled with ice. Stir gently and garnish with an orange slice. This became our go-to drink for early evening relaxation. Light and refreshing, it was perfect for sipping as we watched the sun set over whatever new landscape we found ourselves in.
2. **Desert Bloom Margarita**

- 2 oz Blanco tequila
- 1 oz Fresh lime juice
- 0.5 oz Prickly pear syrup
- 0.5 oz Triple sec
- Prickly pear fruit for garnish

1. *Method:* Shake all ingredients with ice. Strain into a rocks glass filled with fresh ice. Garnish with a slice of prickly pear fruit. Inspired by the surprising bursts of color we encountered in the desert, this bright pink margarita variation became our tribute to the resilient beauty of arid landscapes.
2. **Pacific Northwest Porch Pounder**

- 1.5 oz Gin
- 1 oz Fresh lemon juice
- 0.75 oz Lavender-honey syrup
- 2 oz Soda water
- Fresh lavender sprig for garnish

1. *Method:* Shake gin, lemon juice, and lavender-honey syrup with ice. Strain into a collins glass filled with ice. Top with soda water and garnish with a lavender sprig. This floral, honeyed cooler was our refreshment of choice while exploring the lush landscapes of the Pacific Northwest. It was easy to batch for lazy afternoons spent with new friends.
2. **Roadside Stand Smash**

- 2 oz White rum
- 1 oz Fresh lime juice
- 0.75 oz Simple syrup
- 4-5 Ripe strawberries
- Mint sprig for garnish

1. *Method:* Muddle strawberries in a shaker. Add remaining ingredients and shake with ice. Double strain into a rocks glass filled with crushed ice.

Garnish with a mint sprig. This drink was born from our habit of stopping at roadside fruit stands. The fresh strawberries made each batch unique, reflecting the local terroir of wherever we happened to be.

2. **Beachcomber's Cooler**

- 2 oz Coconut rum
- 1 oz Blue curaçao
- 2 oz Pineapple juice
- 1 oz Cream of coconut
- Pineapple wedge and cherry for garnish

1. *Method:* Blend all ingredients with ice until smooth. Pour into a hurricane glass and garnish with a pineapple wedge and cherry. This tropical sipper was our liquid vacation whenever we found ourselves near a beach. Its playful blue color reminded us of ocean views and carefree summer days.

Tips for Crafting Spring/Summer Cocktails on the Road:

1. **Invest in a good cooler**: Fresh ingredients are key for spring/summer

cocktails. A reliable cooler kept our fruits and herbs fresh even in Priscilla's limited space.

2. **Embrace local, seasonal produce**: We made it a point to visit farmers' markets wherever we went, incorporating local fruits into our cocktails for a true taste of each place we visited.

3. **Pre-batch when possible**: For music festivals or beach days, we'd pre-batch cocktails (minus any carbonated ingredients) in large mason jars for easy serving.

4. **Don't forget the ice**: We learned to plan ahead for our ice needs, especially in hot climates where a cold drink can make all the difference.

5. **Garnish creatively**: When fresh herbs or fruits weren't available, we'd get creative with garnishes, using everything from locally-sourced wildflowers to colorful cocktail umbrellas found in quirky roadside shops.

FALL/WINTER WARMERS - COMFORT IN A CUP

As the leaves began to turn and a chill crept into the air, our cocktail preferences shifted towards richer, warming drinks that could combat the cold and lift our spirits on grey days.

Key Characteristics of Fall/Winter Cocktails:

1. **Dark Base Spirits**: Whiskey, aged rum, brandy, and dark tequila come to the forefront.
2. **Warming Spices**: Cinnamon, nutmeg, clove, and ginger add depth and heat.
3. **Rich Modifiers**: Sweet vermouth, port, and liqueurs like amaretto bring complexity.
4. **Seasonal Produce**: Apples, pears, cranberries, and pumpkin evoke autumnal flavors.
5. **Higher Alcohol Content**: These cocktails often pack more of a punch to warm from within.

Essential Techniques for Fall/Winter Cocktails:

1. **Stirring**: For spirit-forward cocktails that don't require dilution from shaking.

2. **Hot Drink Preparation**: Using hot water or warm milk as a base for toddies and other hot cocktails.
3. **Infusing**: Creating spiced syrups or infused spirits to add layers of flavor.
4. **Flame**: Carefully igniting expressed citrus oils or high-proof spirits for added warmth and aroma.

Featured Cocktail: Tornado Chaser

This cocktail was born from our heart-pounding experience outrunning a tornado in Kansas. It's bold, spicy, and leaves you feeling warm and alive.

Ingredients:

- 2 oz Kansas whiskey
- 4 oz Ginger beer
- 0.5 oz Fresh lime juice
- 2 dashes Angostura bitters
- Candied ginger for garnish

Method: Build in a copper mug or highball glass filled with ice. Stir gently to combine. Garnish with a piece of candied ginger.

The Story: After our close call with a tornado in Kansas, we needed a drink that could calm our nerves and warm our spirits. The local Kansas whiskey grounded the drink in a sense of place, while the spicy kick of ginger beer mimicked the adrenaline rush we'd just experienced. A touch of lime added brightness, like the flash of lightning we'd seen, while the Angostura bitters provided depth and complexity. The result was a cocktail that made us feel both comforted and invigorated - ready to face whatever the road might throw at us next.

A Tornado in Kansas

More Fall/Winter Cocktails from Our Travels:

1. The Autumn Road

- 2 oz Bourbon
- 0.5 oz Apple cider reduction
- 0.25 oz Maple syrup
- 2 dashes Orange bitters
- Cinnamon stick for garnish

1. *Method:* Stir all ingredients with ice. Strain into a rocks glass over a large ice cube. Garnish with a cinnamon stick. This became our go-to drink for chilly evenings around the campfire. The apple and maple flavors captured the essence of fall, while the bourbon kept us warm as temperatures dropped.

1. **Rocky Mountain Warmer**

- 1.5 oz Rye whiskey
- 0.5 oz Yellow Chartreuse
- 0.5 oz Honey syrup
- 4 oz Hot water
- Lemon wheel studded with cloves for garnish

1. *Method:* Build in a mug, stirring to combine. Garnish with a clove-studded

lemon wheel. We crafted this comforting hot toddy variation during a snowstorm in Colorado. The herbal notes of the Chartreuse reminded us of the mountain forests around us.

2. **Cranberry Bog Boulevardier**

- 1.5 oz Bourbon
- 1 oz Campari
- 1 oz Sweet vermouth
- 0.25 oz Cranberry syrup
- Orange twist for garnish

1. *Method:* Stir all ingredients with ice. Strain into a coupe glass. Garnish with an orange twist. Inspired by the cranberry bogs we saw in New England, this autumnal twist on a classic cocktail became our sophisticated evening sipper.

2. **Priscilla's Pumpkin Spice**

- 2 oz Spiced rum
- 1 oz Pumpkin puree
- 0.5 oz Maple syrup
- 0.5 oz Heavy cream
- Nutmeg for garnish

1. *Method:* Shake all ingredients with ice. Strain into a rocks glass filled with fresh ice. Grate fresh nutmeg over the top. Our homemade answer to the ubiquitous pumpkin spice latte, this cocktail kept us cozy on crisp fall mornings (don't judge - we weren't driving those days!).

2. **Smoked Sage Old Fashioned**

- 2 oz Rye whiskey
- 0.25 oz Maple syrup
- 2 dashes Black walnut bitters
- Smoked sage leaf for garnish

1. *Method:* Stir whiskey, maple syrup, and bitters with ice. Strain into a rocks glass over a large ice cube. Garnish with a smoked sage leaf. We created this smoky, herbaceous cocktail after a day of hiking through sage-covered hills. The aroma instantly transported us back to the trail.

Tips for Crafting Fall/Winter Cocktails on the Road:

1. **Invest in good thermoses**: For hot cocktails, a quality thermos kept our drinks warm even on the coldest nights.
2. **Spice it up**: We kept a small kit of whole spices for mulling cider or wine, adding instant warmth to any drink.
3. **Embrace local spirits**: Wherever we went, we sought out local distilleries for unique whiskeys, brandies, or other spirits that could form the base of our cold-weather cocktails.
4. **Don't forget the classics**: Sometimes, a well-made hot toddy or Irish coffee was all we needed to ward off the chill.
5. **Get creative with hot water sources**: When camping, we'd use hot water from our campfire kettle to make warming cocktails under the stars.

Drinking in the Seasons

As we reflect on our journey through the seasons, we're struck by how our cocktail choices mirrored the changing world around us. From the light, bright flavors of spring and summer to the rich, warming concoctions of fall and winter, each drink was a liquid snapshot of a particular time and place.

These seasonal cocktails taught us to be

present in the moment, to appreciate the unique gifts that each time of year brings. They showed us how to adapt to our environment, making the most of local, seasonal ingredients wherever we found ourselves.

Most importantly, crafting these drinks reminded us that the joy of the journey isn't just in the destination, but in how we choose to experience each moment along the way. Whether we were cooling off with a Coachella Sunset under the blazing summer sun or warming up with a Tornado Chaser on a blustery autumn evening, each sip was a celebration of where we were and when we were there.

As you embark on your own adventures, we encourage you to let the seasons guide your cocktail choices. Embrace the fresh, vibrant flavors of spring and summer, and find comfort in the rich, warming drinks of fall and winter. Let each cocktail be a reflection of your surroundings, a liquid postcard from wherever your journey takes you.

After all, isn't that what the spirit of a Post Modern Gypsy is all about? Adapting to your environment, making the most of what's available, and always finding a way to raise a glass to the adventure at hand.

NON-ALCOHOLIC COCKTAILS: SPIRITED ADVENTURES WITHOUT THE SPIRITS

As we journeyed across the country in our trusty Priscilla, we quickly realized that the art of crafting delicious drinks wasn't limited to those containing alcohol. Whether it was for the designated driver, those who chose not to drink, or simply for times when we wanted to enjoy a crafted beverage without the effects of alcohol, non-alcoholic cocktails - or mocktails - became an essential part of our mobile bar repertoire.

The Rise of Mocktail Culture

In recent years, there's been a significant shift in drinking culture, with more people seeking out high-quality, non-alcoholic options. This trend aligns perfectly with the spirit of inclusive adventure that guided our journey. We found that the best experiences were those shared by all, regardless of their drinking preferences.

Key Elements of a Great Mocktail:

1. **Complexity**: Like their alcoholic counterparts, great mocktails should have depth and layers of flavor.
2. **Balance**: The interplay of sweet, sour, bitter, and savory elements is crucial.

3. **Texture**: Techniques like muddling, shaking with ice, or adding carbonation can create interesting textures.
4. **Presentation**: A well-garnished mocktail can be just as visually appealing as any cocktail.
5. **Creativity**: Unique ingredients and unexpected combinations keep things interesting.

Essential Ingredients for Mocktail Making

During our travels, we discovered a range of ingredients that became staples in our non-alcoholic creations:

1. **Fresh Juices**: Nothing beats the flavor of freshly squeezed citrus or pressed apple juice.
2. **Herbs and Spices**: Mint, basil, rosemary, and cinnamon added depth and aroma.
3. **Bitters**: Many bitters are non-alcoholic and can add complexity to mocktails.
4. **Syrups**: Both store-bought and homemade syrups allowed us to add sweetness and flavor.
5. **Carbonated Mixers**: Soda water, tonic, and ginger beer added fizz and flavor.

6. **Tea**: Both hot and cold teas served as excellent mocktail bases.
7. **Non-Alcoholic Spirits**: We experimented with brands like Seedlip and Ritual, which mimic the flavors of traditional spirits without the alcohol.

Featured Mocktail: Virgin Sweet Tea Wanderer

Our "Sweet Tea Wanderer" cocktail became a favorite during our travels, but we wanted to create a version that everyone could enjoy. Here's our non-alcoholic take on this Southern-inspired classic:

Ingredients:

- 2 oz Strong-brewed black tea, chilled
- 1 oz Fresh lemon juice
- 0.75 oz Honey syrup (equal parts honey and hot water, cooled)
- 2-3 Fresh mint leaves
- Soda water
- Lemon wheel and mint sprig for garnish

Method: In a shaker, muddle the mint leaves with the honey syrup. Add the chilled tea and lemon juice. Fill with ice and shake vigorously.

Strain into a highball glass filled with fresh ice. Top with soda water. Garnish with a lemon wheel and mint sprig.

The Story: This mocktail captures the essence of lazy Southern afternoons and the refreshing simplicity of sweet tea. The strong tea base provides a robust flavor that stands in for the missing alcohol, while the lemon adds brightness and the honey brings sweetness. The mint and soda water keep it light and refreshing, perfect for sipping on warm days as the landscape rolls by.

More Mocktails Inspired by Our Travels

1. **Desert Sunrise**

- 2 oz Fresh orange juice
- 1 oz Prickly pear syrup
- 0.5 oz Fresh lime juice
- Soda water
- Orange slice and prickly pear fruit for garnish

1. *Method:* Shake juices and syrup with ice. Strain into a sunrise glass over fresh ice. Top with soda water. Garnish with an orange slice and prickly pear fruit. Inspired by the vibrant colors of a Southwestern sunrise, this mocktail

became our go-to morning refresher in the desert regions.

2. **Pacific Northwest Mist**

- 2 oz Apple juice
- 0.5 oz Fresh lemon juice
- 0.5 oz Lavender syrup
- 2 dashes Non-alcoholic aromatic bitters
- Soda water
- Apple slice and lavender sprig for garnish

1. *Method:* Shake all ingredients except soda water with ice. Strain into a highball glass over fresh ice. Top with soda water. Garnish with an apple slice and lavender sprig. This mocktail captures the crisp, floral essence of the Pacific Northwest. We often enjoyed it while watching fog roll in over evergreen forests.

2. **Roadside Stand Lemonade**

- 2 oz Fresh lemonade
- 1 oz Strawberry puree
- 0.5 oz Vanilla syrup
- 2-3 Basil leaves
- Soda water

- Strawberry and basil leaf for garnish

1. *Method:* Muddle basil leaves in a shaker. Add lemonade, strawberry puree, and vanilla syrup. Shake with ice. Strain into a mason jar filled with crushed ice. Top with soda water. Garnish with a strawberry and basil leaf. Inspired by the bounty of roadside fruit stands, this elevated lemonade became our refreshment of choice on hot summer days.
2. **Mountain Meadow Fizz**

- 1.5 oz Seedlip Garden 108
- 0.75 oz Fresh lemon juice
- 0.5 oz Honey syrup
- 2-3 Cucumber slices
- Soda water
- Cucumber ribbon and edible flower for garnish

1. *Method:* Muddle cucumber slices in a shaker. Add Seedlip, lemon juice, and honey syrup. Shake with ice. Double strain into a collins glass filled with fresh ice. Top with soda water. Garnish with a cucumber ribbon and edible

flower. This mocktail, with its garden-fresh flavors, reminded us of wildflower-filled mountain meadows we encountered in our travels.

2. **Smoky Sunset Sipper**

- 2 oz Fresh grapefruit juice
- 0.5 oz Fresh lime juice
- 0.5 oz Agave syrup
- 2-3 drops Liquid smoke
- Chili salt for rimming
- Grapefruit wedge for garnish

1. *Method:* Rim a rocks glass with chili salt. Shake all ingredients with ice. Strain into the prepared glass over fresh ice. Garnish with a grapefruit wedge. Inspired by the smoky sunsets we witnessed in the Southwest, this mocktail brings together citrus, sweetness, and a hint of smoke for a complex, non-alcoholic sipper.

Techniques for Elevating Mocktails

Throughout our journey, we discovered several techniques that helped us create mocktails that were just as satisfying as their alcoholic counterparts:

1. **Layering**: By carefully pouring ingredients of different densities, we created visually striking mocktails with distinct layers of flavor.
2. **Muddling**: This technique allowed us to extract maximum flavor from fresh fruits and herbs.
3. **Infusions**: We often infused water or syrups with herbs, spices, or fruit to add depth to our mocktails.
4. **Garnishing**: We learned that an impressive garnish can elevate a simple mocktail into a memorable experience.
5. **Smoke**: Using a smoking gun or burning herbs added an intriguing smoky element to some of our creations.
6. **Fermentation**: We experimented with making our own kombucha and kefir, which added complex, fermented flavors to our mocktails.

The Art of Mocktail and Food Pairing

Just like cocktails, we found that mocktails could be expertly paired with food to enhance the overall dining experience. Here are some pairings we discovered:

- Our Virgin Sweet Tea Wanderer paired beautifully with spicy Southern barbecue, the sweetness and acidity balancing out the heat and richness of the food.
- The Desert Sunrise was a perfect match for a hearty Southwest breakfast burrito, its bright flavors cutting through the savory dish.
- Pacific Northwest Mist complemented a salmon dish wonderfully, its apple and lavender notes enhancing the fish's delicate flavor.

Mocktails for Every Occasion

We found that having a repertoire of mocktails allowed us to create the right drink for any situation:

- **Morning Refreshers**: Light, fruity mocktails often featuring citrus or green tea.
- **Afternoon Pick-Me-Ups**: More complex mocktails with herbs and spices to awaken the palate.
- **Evening Sophistication**: Rich, layered mocktails that could stand in for traditional cocktails at social gatherings.

- **Nightcaps**: Warm, soothing mocktails featuring flavors like vanilla, cinnamon, or chamomile.

The Importance of Inclusivity in Drinking Culture

Our journey taught us the value of having great non-alcoholic options available. Whether it was to accommodate those who don't drink alcohol, to ensure everyone could participate in our cocktail experiments, or simply to pace ourselves on long evenings of socializing, mocktails played a crucial role in our travel experience.

We found that offering thoughtful, well-crafted mocktails alongside our cocktails made our impromptu gatherings more inclusive and enjoyable for everyone. It allowed all of our fellow travelers to feel part of the experience, regardless of their relationship with alcohol.

The Spirit of Adventure in Every Sip

As we reflect on our mocktail journey, we're struck by how these non-alcoholic creations embodied the very spirit of our travels. Like our decision to hit the road in Priscilla, crafting mocktails is about thinking creatively, making the most of available ingredients, and finding joy in the process of discovery and creation.

These drinks taught us that you don't need alcohol to capture a sense of place, to celebrate a moment, or to create a memorable experience. From the sun-soaked deserts of the Southwest to the misty forests of the Pacific Northwest, our mocktails allowed us to bottle up the essence of each place we visited, creating liquid postcards that could be enjoyed by anyone.

Most importantly, our foray into mocktails reminded us that the best journeys are those that can be shared by all. By ensuring we always had delicious, non-alcoholic options available, we were able to create a more inclusive, welcoming atmosphere wherever we went.

As you embark on your own adventures, we encourage you to embrace the world of mocktails. Challenge yourself to create drinks that are just as complex, balanced, and satisfying as any cocktail. Let your mocktails tell the story of your journey, capture the essence of the places you visit, and bring people together in celebration of the adventure at hand.

After all, isn't that what the spirit of a Post Modern Gypsy is all about? Finding joy in creativity, inclusivity, and the endless possibilities that each new day brings - with or without alcohol in your glass.

SYRUPS, BITTERS, AND INFUSIONS: CAPTURING FLAVORS OF THE JOURNEY

As we traversed the country in our trusty Priscilla, we discovered that the secret to truly unique and memorable cocktails often lay in the homemade ingredients we crafted along the way. Syrups, bitters, and infusions became our liquid souvenirs, allowing us to capture the essence of each place we visited and incorporate it into our drinks. This section explores the art of creating these fundamental cocktail components, with a special focus on how our travels inspired new and exciting flavors.

THE BASICS OF HOMEMADE COCKTAIL INGREDIENTS

SYRUPS: SWEET FOUNDATIONS

Syrups are the sweeteners of the cocktail world, but they can be so much more than just sugar water. By infusing syrups with herbs, spices, fruits, or even vegetables, we were able to add layers of flavor to our drinks.

Basic Simple Syrup Recipe:

- 1 cup water
- 1 cup granulated sugar

Method: Combine water and sugar in a saucepan over medium heat. Stir until sugar dissolves completely. Remove from heat and let cool.

Store in a clean, airtight container in the refrigerator for up to one month.

Tip: For rich simple syrup, use a 2:1 ratio of sugar to water.

Bitters: Aromatic Enhancers

Bitters are highly concentrated flavor extracts that add depth and complexity to cocktails. While many commercial bitters are available, creating our own allowed us to experiment with unique flavor combinations.

Basic Bitters Recipe:

- 2 cups high-proof neutral spirit (like vodka)
- 2-3 tablespoons dried bittering agent (like gentian root or cinchona bark)
- 2-3 tablespoons aromatic herbs and spices
- 1-2 tablespoons fresh citrus peel

Method: Combine all ingredients in a glass jar. Seal and store in a cool, dark place for 2-4 weeks, shaking daily. Strain through cheesecloth and store in a dropper bottle.

Tip: The possibilities for bitters flavors are endless. We often used local herbs or spices to create bitters that captured the essence of each place we visited.

Infusions: Spirit Transformers

Infusions allow you to impart new flavors into base spirits, creating unique ingredients for cocktails. The process is simple, but the results can be extraordinary.

Basic Infusion Method:

- 750ml base spirit (vodka, gin, rum, etc.)
- Flavoring ingredients (fruits, herbs, spices, etc.)

Method: Add flavoring ingredients to the spirit in a clean glass jar. Seal and store in a cool, dark place. Infusion times vary: herbs may only need a day or two, while fruits can take a week or more. Taste regularly and strain when desired flavor is achieved.

Tip: Start with small batches to experiment with flavors and infusion times.

RECIPES FOR HOMEMADE INGREDIENTS
SYRUPS

1. **Lavender Honey Syrup**

- 1 cup water
- 1 cup honey
- 2 tablespoons dried lavender buds

1. *Method:* Bring water to a boil, remove from heat and add honey and lavender. Stir until honey dissolves. Let steep for 30 minutes, then strain and cool. *Inspired by:* Fields of wild lavender we encountered in the Pacific Northwest.
2. **Smoked Rosemary Syrup**

- 1 cup water
- 1 cup sugar
- 2-3 sprigs fresh rosemary
- Wood chips for smoking

1. *Method:* Smoke rosemary sprigs for 5-10 minutes. Make simple syrup, then add smoked rosemary and let steep for 30 minutes. Strain and cool. *Inspired by:* Campfires in the mountains of Colorado.
2. **Prickly Pear Syrup**

- 1 cup prickly pear juice (from about 2-3 prickly pears)
- 1 cup sugar

1. *Method:* Blend prickly pears and strain to get juice. Combine juice and sugar in a saucepan, heat until sugar dissolves. Cool and store. *Inspired by:* The vibrant colors of the Sonoran Desert.

Bitters

1. **Desert Sage Bitters**

- 2 cups high-proof vodka

- 1/4 cup dried sage leaves
- 1 tablespoon dried gentian root
- 1 cinnamon stick
- 3 cardamom pods
- Peel of 1 orange

1. *Method:* Combine all ingredients in a jar. Let infuse for 2 weeks, shaking daily. Strain and store in a dropper bottle. *Inspired by:* The aromatic sage brush of the high desert.
2. **Autumn Spice Bitters**

- 2 cups high-proof vodka
- 1 tablespoon dried gentian root
- 1 vanilla bean, split
- 2 cinnamon sticks
- 5 whole cloves
- 1/4 cup dried apple chips
- Peel of 1 lemon

1. *Method:* Combine all ingredients in a jar. Let infuse for 3 weeks, shaking daily. Strain and store in a dropper bottle. *Inspired by:* The warm, spicy scents of autumn in New England.

Infusions

1. **Wildflower Gin**

- 750ml gin
- 1 cup mixed edible wildflowers (like violets, marigolds, and pansies)

1. *Method:* Add flowers to gin in a clean jar. Infuse for 24 hours, then strain and rebottle. *Inspired by:* Meadows bursting with wildflowers in the Rocky Mountains.
2. **Pecan Bourbon**

- 750ml bourbon
- 1 cup toasted pecans, roughly chopped

1. *Method:* Add pecans to bourbon in a clean jar. Infuse for 5-7 days, shaking daily. Strain and rebottle. *Inspired by:*Pecan groves in the South and the rich tradition of Southern bourbon.

SPOTLIGHT - CREATING FLAVORS INSPIRED BY TRAVEL EXPERIENCES

Our journey across America was not just a visual feast, but a sensory adventure that engaged all of our senses, especially taste and smell. We found ourselves constantly inspired to capture the essence of our experiences in liquid form. Here are some of the most memorable flavor creations from our travels:

1. Route 66 Root Beer Syrup

As we traveled along stretches of the historic Route 66, we were struck by the nostalgia evoked by old-fashioned diners and their classic root beer floats. This inspired us to create our own root beer syrup, perfect for adding a touch of Americana to cocktails.

Recipe:

- 2 cups water
- 2 cups sugar
- 2 tablespoons sassafras root bark
- 1 vanilla bean, split
- 1 cinnamon stick
- 1 star anise
- 1/4 teaspoon food-grade sarsaparilla root

Method: Combine all ingredients in a saucepan. Bring to a boil, then reduce heat and simmer for 15 minutes. Remove from heat and let steep for 1 hour. Strain and cool.

This syrup became the star ingredient in our "Route 66 Float" cocktail, featuring bourbon, root beer syrup, and a splash of cream, garnished with a maraschino cherry.

2. Pacific Coast Highway Fog Bitters

Driving along the Pacific Coast Highway, we were mesmerized by the ethereal fog rolling in from the ocean. The misty, salt-tinged air inspired us to create bitters that captured this unique coastal atmosphere.

Recipe:

- 2 cups high-proof vodka

- 1 tablespoon dried gentian root
- 1 tablespoon dried sea kelp
- 1 tablespoon juniper berries
- Peel of 1 lemon
- 1/2 teaspoon sea salt

Method: Combine all ingredients in a jar. Let infuse for 3 weeks, shaking daily. Strain and store in a dropper bottle.

These bitters added a subtle maritime note to our gin-based "Coastal Fog Martini," enhancing the drink with hints of the sea.

3. Zion Sunset Infused Tequila

The breathtaking sunsets in Zion National Park, with their vibrant oranges, reds, and purples, inspired us to create a visually striking and flavorful infused tequila.

Recipe:

- 750ml silver tequila
- 1 dragon fruit, sliced
- 1 blood orange, sliced
- 1/4 cup dried hibiscus flowers

Method: Combine all ingredients in a large glass jar. Infuse for 48 hours, then strain and rebottle.

This beautifully colored tequila became the

base for our "Zion Sunset Margarita," garnished with a dehydrated blood orange wheel.

4. Bourbon Street Jazz Bitters

The lively, spicy, and slightly mysterious atmosphere of New Orleans' Bourbon Street inspired a complex, jazz-like blend of bitters.

Recipe:

- 2 cups high-proof vodka
- 1 tablespoon dried gentian root
- 1 vanilla bean, split
- 2 whole allspice berries
- 2 whole cloves
- 1 small piece of star anise
- 1/4 teaspoon cayenne pepper
- Peel of 1 orange

Method: Combine all ingredients in a jar. Let infuse for 4 weeks, shaking daily. Strain and store in a dropper bottle.

These bitters added depth and complexity to our "Bourbon Street Sazerac," bringing a taste of New Orleans to wherever we happened to be parked.

5. Appalachian Apple Pie Syrup

Driving through the Appalachian Mountains in autumn, we were charmed by the abundance of apple orchards and the prevalence of homemade apple pies. This inspired a syrup that captured the essence of this all-American dessert.

Recipe:

- 2 cups apple cider
- 1 cup brown sugar
- 2 cinnamon sticks
- 1 vanilla bean, split
- 5 whole cloves
- 1/4 teaspoon nutmeg

Method: Combine all ingredients in a saucepan. Bring to a boil, then reduce heat and simmer for 20 minutes until slightly thickened. Strain and cool.

This syrup became the key ingredient in our "Appalachian Apple Pie Flip," a comforting cocktail perfect for cool mountain evenings.

Conclusion: The Alchemy of Experience

Creating our own syrups, bitters, and infusions became a form of liquid alchemy, allowing us to transform our travel experiences into tangible (and tastable) memories. Each bottle in our mobile bar told a story - of a place we'd been, a sight we'd seen, or a person we'd met.

These homemade ingredients did more than just flavor our cocktails; they allowed us to share our journey with others in a unique and immersive way. A sip of a cocktail made with our Route 66 Root Beer Syrup could transport fellow travelers back to the heyday of American road trips, while our Pacific Coast Highway Fog Bitters could evoke the misty magic of the California coastline.

Moreover, the process of creating these ingredients taught us to be more observant and appreciative of the world around us. We found ourselves paying closer attention to the native plants in each region, the local culinary traditions, and even the quality of light and air in different landscapes. Our journey became not just about seeing new places, but about deeply experiencing them through all our senses.

As you embark on your own adventures, we encourage you to consider how you might capture the essence of your experiences in liquid form. Whether it's a syrup inspired by a local fruit, bitters that evoke a memorable landscape, or an infusion that captures the spirit of a city, these homemade ingredients can become lasting souvenirs of your journey.

Remember, the beauty of creating your own cocktail ingredients is that there are no hard and fast rules. Let your experiences guide you, trust your palate, and don't be afraid to experiment. After all, isn't that what the spirit of a Post Modern Gypsy is all about? Finding inspiration in the world around you, creating something unique, and sharing it with others along the way.

So here's to the syrups that sweeten our memories, the bitters that add depth to our experiences, and the infusions that transform the ordinary into the extraordinary. May your travels be flavorful, your creations be inspired, and your cocktails always tell a story.

GARNISHES AND PRESENTATION: THE ART OF LIQUID CANVAS

As our journey progressed and Priscilla transformed from a simple camper into a rolling work of art, we found ourselves inspired to bring that same creative spirit to our cocktails. We realized that a drink is not just about taste, but also about visual appeal and the story it tells. In this section, we'll explore how we elevated our cocktail game through creative garnishes and presentation, turning each drink into a miniature work of art.

The Evolution of Our Garnish Philosophy

At the beginning of our journey, our garnishes were simple and functional - a twist of citrus peel here, a sprig of mint there. But as Priscilla's exterior became more vibrant and expressive, we felt compelled to match that energy in our drinks. We began to see each cocktail as a blank canvas, waiting to be adorned with edible art.

Our garnish philosophy evolved to embody several key principles:

1. **Reflect the drink's flavors**: Each garnish should complement or enhance the flavors in the glass.
2. **Tell a story**: Like Priscilla's painted exterior, our garnishes began to narrate our journey and experiences.
3. **Engage the senses**: Beyond taste, we aimed to create garnishes that appealed to sight, smell, and sometimes even touch.
4. **Sustainability**: We tried to use every part of our ingredients, reducing waste and creating unique garnishes in the process.
5. **Interactivity**: Some of our garnishes became part of the drinking experience, changing the flavor of the cocktail as you sipped.

Creative Garnishes Inspired by Priscilla's Transformation

1. **The Quotation Wheel**: Inspired by the quotes painted on Priscilla's side, we created edible rice paper strips with food-safe ink, each bearing a quote from our travels. These were clipped to the rim of the glass with a tiny clothespin, allowing drinkers to read a new quote with each sip.

2. **Sculptural Ice**: We began freezing flowers, herbs, and even miniature landscapes into large ice spheres. As the ice melted, it slowly revealed these hidden elements, changing the drink's appearance and flavor over time.

3. **The Painted Rim**: Using edible dust and gel food coloring, we painted intricate designs on the rims of glasses, mirroring the artistic style of Priscilla's exterior.

4. **Dehydrated Fruit Mosaics**: We dehydrated thin slices of various fruits and arranged them into colorful mosaics that floated on top of cocktails, reminiscent of the patchwork designs on Priscilla.

5. **Aromatic Smoke Bubbles**: Using a combination of flavored smoke and bubble solution, we created delicate,

scented bubbles that floated on top of cocktails, bursting with aromatic essence when touched.

6. **Edible Flower Arrangements**: Inspired by the wildflowers we encountered on our travels, we began creating miniature, edible flower arrangements as garnishes, each telling the story of a specific location.

7. **The Spice Road**: For some of our more complex cocktails, we created a "spice road" down the side of the glass using different colored spices and herbs, allowing drinkers to customize their experience by incorporating these elements as they sipped.

Presentation Techniques

Our presentation evolved alongside our garnish game. Here are some techniques we developed:

1. **Vintage Glassware**: We collected unique, vintage glasses from thrift stores across the country, each with its own history and character.

2. **Repurposed Vessels**: In the spirit of Priscilla's transformation, we

repurposed items found on our travels into unconventional cocktail vessels - think hollowed-out books, antique oil lamps, or even small travel souvenirs.

3. **Themed Serve Ware**: We created custom coasters, stirrers, and picks that matched the theme of each cocktail, often incorporating found objects from our travels.

4. **Theatrical Presentation**: Some cocktails were presented with a bit of tableside theater - for instance, pouring a vibrant syrup over a scaffold of cotton candy, or cracking open a smoked cloche to release aromas.

5. **Interactive Elements**: We introduced elements that encouraged interaction, like DIY garnish stations or cocktails that required assembly by the drinker.

Featured Cocktail: "Painted Lady Priscilla"

This cocktail is our liquid tribute to Priscilla's transformation into a vibrant, rolling work of art. It's a visually striking drink that captures the spirit of our journey and the joy of creative expression.

Ingredients:

- 1.5 oz Pink gin
- 0.5 oz Elderflower liqueur
- 1 oz Fresh grapefruit juice
- Prosecco float
- Edible paint swirl (made with flavored syrups and edible glitter)

Glassware: Clear champagne flute
Method:

1. In a shaker, combine pink gin, elderflower liqueur, and grapefruit juice with ice. Shake vigorously.
2. Strain into a chilled champagne flute.
3. Slowly float Prosecco on top.
4. Using a thin brush or dropper, create a swirl of edible paint on the surface of the drink. We use a combination of flavored syrups (like raspberry, passion fruit, and blue curaçao) mixed with edible glitter to create vibrant, shimmering colors.

Garnish: A dehydrated grapefruit wheel, half-dipped in pink edible glitter, balanced on the rim of the glass.

Presentation: The cocktail is served on a custom coaster featuring a miniature reproduction of one of Priscilla's painted panels. A small artist's palette filled with additional edible paints and a tiny brush is provided alongside, allowing the drinker to add their own artistic touches to the drink.

The Experience: As you sip the "Painted Lady Priscilla," the flavors evolve much like our journey. The initial taste is bright and zesty from the grapefruit and gin, followed by the floral notes of elderflower. The Prosecco adds a celebratory effervescence. As you drink, the edible paint on top creates ever-changing patterns, making each sip visually unique. The dehydrated grapefruit wheel can be nibbled on between sips, adding a concentrated burst of citrus flavor.

This cocktail encapsulates our philosophy that a drink should be a multi-sensory experience. It engages sight with its vibrant colors and swirling patterns, smell with the aromatic gin and elderflower, taste with its complex flavor profile, touch with the different textures of the glass and garnish, and even sound with the gentle fizz of the Prosecco.

Conclusion: Painting with Liquid Colors

As Priscilla evolved from a simple camper into a masterpiece on wheels, our cocktails underwent a parallel transformation. We learned that garnishes and presentation are not just final touches, but integral parts of the cocktail experience. They're a way to tell a story, evoke a memory, or transport the drinker to a specific time and place.

Our journey taught us that creativity knows no bounds. Whether you're painting a camper or crafting a cocktail, the most important ingredients are imagination and a willingness to experiment. We encourage you to look at each drink as a potential canvas, waiting for your unique artistic touch.

Remember, the goal isn't perfection, but expression. Just as Priscilla's painted exterior told the story of our travels, let your garnishes and presentation choices reflect your own journey, wherever it may take you. After all, in the world of a Post Modern Gypsy, life itself is art - why should our cocktails be any different?

FOOD PAIRING AND COCKTAIL PARTIES: A CULINARY ROAD TRIP

s we traversed the country in our trusty Priscilla, we discovered that the joy of a well-crafted cocktail is often amplified when paired with the right food. Our journey became as much a culinary adventure as a mixological one, as we explored regional cuisines and local flavors. In this section, we'll share our insights on pairing cocktails with the diverse foods we encountered, and guide you through hosting your own Post Modern Gypsy themed party.

PAIRING COCKTAILS WITH REGIONAL CUISINES

Our cross-country journey exposed us to a rich tapestry of regional American cuisines. We found that pairing local dishes with thoughtfully crafted cocktails not only enhanced the dining experience but also deepened our connection to each place we visited. Here are some of our favorite pairings from different regions:

The Southwest

The bold, spicy flavors of Southwestern cuisine called for cocktails that could stand up to the heat while providing refreshing relief.

Pairing: Green Chile Cheeseburger with a Prickly Pear Margarita

- The Dish: A New Mexico classic, featuring a juicy beef patty topped with roasted green chiles and melted cheese.
- The Cocktail: Our Prickly Pear Margarita, made with silver tequila, lime juice, and homemade prickly pear syrup.
- Why it Works: The sweet-tart flavors of the prickly pear and the coolness of the margarita provide a perfect counterpoint to the spicy, savory burger. The tequila's earthy notes complement the roasted chiles beautifully.

The Pacific Northwest

The fresh, often delicate flavors of Pacific Northwest cuisine paired wonderfully with cocktails that highlighted local ingredients and matched the region's often misty, ethereal atmosphere.

Pairing: Cedar-Planked Salmon with a Rainier Cherry Gin Fizz

- The Dish: Wild-caught salmon, slow-cooked on a cedar plank to infuse it with a subtle woodsy flavor.
- The Cocktail: A gin fizz featuring locally distilled gin, muddled Rainier cherries,

lemon juice, and a splash of soda water.

- Why it Works: The bright, fruity notes of the cocktail complement the rich, oily salmon without overpowering it. The gin's botanical notes echo the cedar flavor in the fish.

The Deep South

Southern cuisine, with its bold flavors and hearty portions, called for cocktails that could hold their own without overwhelming the palate.

Pairing: Shrimp and Grits with a Peach Bourbon Smash

- The Dish: Creamy stone-ground grits topped with succulent shrimp in a spicy, garlicky sauce.
- The Cocktail: Our Peach Bourbon Smash, featuring bourbon, muddled fresh peaches, lemon juice, and a touch of honey.
- Why it Works: The sweetness of the peach and the warmth of the bourbon stand up to the rich, spicy shrimp while complementing the creamy grits. The hint of honey ties everything together.

New England

The coastal cuisine of New England, with its focus on fresh seafood, paired beautifully with crisp, clean cocktails that evoked the region's maritime heritage.

Pairing: Lobster Roll with a Cape Codder Reimagined

- The Dish: Chunks of sweet lobster meat lightly dressed with mayo and served in a buttered, toasted roll.
- The Cocktail: Our reimagined Cape Codder, featuring vodka, fresh cranberry juice, a splash of elderflower liqueur, and a rosemary sprig.
- Why it Works: The tartness of the cranberry cuts through the richness of the lobster and mayo, while the elderflower adds a subtle floral note that enhances the lobster's sweetness. The rosemary provides an aromatic element that ties into New England's coastal pine forests.

The Midwest

Midwestern comfort food, hearty and satisfying, called for cocktails with depth and complexity to match.

Pairing: Chicago-Style Deep Dish Pizza with a Lake Michigan Breeze

- The Dish: A thick, cheesy pizza with a robust tomato sauce and a buttery crust.
- The Cocktail: Our Lake Michigan Breeze, featuring gin, Luxardo maraschino liqueur, fresh lime juice, and a splash of violet liqueur.
- Why it Works: The herbal notes of the gin and the tartness of the lime cut through the richness of the cheese and sauce, while the hint of violet adds an unexpected floral note that refreshes the palate between bites.

HOSTING A POST MODERN GYPSY THEMED PARTY

Inspired by our travels and the spirit of adventure that fueled our journey, we've put together a guide to hosting your own Post Modern Gypsy themed cocktail party. This is your chance to take your guests on a cross-country road trip, all from the comfort of your home (or backyard, or rooftop, or wherever your nomadic spirit leads you).

Setting the Scene

1. **Décor:**

- Transform your space into a bohemian traveler's paradise. Use colorful tapestries, vintage maps, and string lights to create a warm, inviting atmosphere.

- Incorporate elements that evoke the open road: vintage suitcases, old license plates, or even a steering wheel as wall art.
- If you have the space, set up a small tent or canopy to create a cozy "camping" corner.

1. **Music**:

- Create a playlist that captures the spirit of the American road trip. Mix classic road trip songs with contemporary indie folk for a perfect Post Modern Gypsy vibe.

1. **Serving Ware**:

- Use a mix of vintage glasses and mason jars for drinks.
- Serve food on enamel camping plates or in creative containers like miniature picnic baskets or tackle boxes.

The Menu

Create a cross-country culinary experience by offering a variety of small bites inspired by different regions:

1. **Southwest Station**:

- Mini green chile cheeseburger sliders
- Elote cups (Mexican street corn in individual servings)
- Paired Cocktail: Prickly Pear Margaritas

1. **Pacific Northwest Corner**:

- Cedar plank salmon bites
- Mini cups of clam chowder
- Paired Cocktail: Rainier Cherry Gin Fizz

1. **Southern Comfort**:

- Shrimp and grits spoons
- Mini pecan pies
- Paired Cocktail: Peach Bourbon Smash

1. **New England Nook**:

- Mini lobster rolls
- Clam cakes

- Paired Cocktail: Cape Codder Reimagined

1. **Midwest Munchies**:

- Deep dish pizza bites
- Miniature cheese and sausage boards
- Paired Cocktail: Lake Michigan Breeze

Interactive Elements

Make your party an immersive experience with these interactive elements:

1. **Cocktail Road Map**: Create a "road map" of cocktails, encouraging guests to "travel" across the country by trying different regional drinks. Provide a small passport-style booklet for guests to collect stamps or stickers for each cocktail they try.
2. **DIY Garnish Station**: Set up a station where guests can garnish their own cocktails with an array of fruits, herbs, and edible flowers. Include some of the creative garnishes inspired by Priscilla's transformation.
3. **Polaroid Guest Book**: Provide a Polaroid camera and encourage guests

to take photos throughout the night. These can be added to a scrapbook-style guest book, along with notes about their favorite cocktails or "travel" memories from the party.

4. **Souvenir Station**: Create a small "gift shop" where guests can take home party favors like mini bottles of infused spirits, packets of custom spice blends, or postcards featuring cocktail recipes.

5. **Campfire Stories**: If you're hosting outdoors, set up a fire pit (or indoor equivalent) and encourage guests to share their own road trip stories or dreams of future adventures.

Signature Cocktails

In addition to the regional pairings, offer these signature cocktails that capture the essence of the Post Modern Gypsy journey:

1. **The Open Road**

- 2 oz Bourbon
- 0.75 oz Fresh lemon juice
- 0.5 oz Honey syrup
- 2 dashes Orange bitters
- Top with ginger beer

- Garnish: Lemon wheel and a sprig of thyme

1. This refreshing, slightly spicy cocktail evokes the excitement of setting out on a new adventure.
2. **Starry Night Sipper**

- 1.5 oz Vodka
- 0.5 oz Blue Curaçao
- 0.75 oz Fresh lime juice
- 0.5 oz Simple syrup
- Top with tonic water
- Garnish: Edible silver stars

1. A nod to nights spent stargazing in the desert, this cocktail's deep blue color is reminiscent of the night sky.
2. **Priscilla's Paint Job**

- 1.5 oz White rum
- 1 oz Coconut cream
- 1 oz Pineapple juice
- 0.5 oz Blue Curaçao
- 0.5 oz Grenadine
- Garnish: Pineapple frond and a cocktail umbrella

1. Inspired by Priscilla's colorful exterior, this layered cocktail is as visually striking as it is delicious.

Tips for Hosting

1. **Pace Your Guests**: With multiple cocktails on offer, encourage responsible enjoyment. Provide water stations and non-alcoholic options.
2. **Prepare in Advance**: Batch cocktails where possible and prep garnishes ahead of time to minimize bartending duties during the party.
3. **Create a Cozy Space**: Ensure there are plenty of comfortable seating areas where guests can relax and chat, mimicking the casual atmosphere of a campsite or roadside diner.
4. **Encourage Exploration**: Just as our journey was about discovery, encourage your guests to try new flavors and combinations.
5. **Share the Stories**: As you serve each cocktail or dish, share a brief anecdote about its inspiration or the region it represents. This adds depth to the experience and sparks conversation.

6. **End the Night with a Nightcap**: As the party winds down, offer a special nightcap like a smoky mezcal old fashioned or a warm, spiced bourbon milk punch to send your guests off with sweet dreams of the open road.

Conclusion: The Journey Continues

Hosting a Post Modern Gypsy themed party is more than just serving drinks and food; it's about creating an experience that captures the spirit of adventure, discovery, and connection that defined our journey. It's an opportunity to take your guests on a virtual road trip, allowing them to explore the diverse flavors and cultures of America without leaving your home.

Remember, the best parties, like the best road trips, are about the journey, not just the destination. Encourage your guests to mingle, share stories, and create new memories. Let the flavors of each cocktail and dish transport them to different parts of the country, sparking conversations about past travels or dreams of future adventures.

As you raise a glass with your friends, take a moment to appreciate the beautiful diversity of American cuisine and cocktail culture. From the zesty flavors of the Southwest to the fresh tastes of the Pacific Northwest, from the comfort foods of the Midwest to the seafood delights of New England, each sip and bite is a celebration of the rich culinary landscape we were fortunate enough to explore.

So here's to good food, great drinks, and the enduring spirit of the open road. May your Post Modern Gypsy party be filled with laughter, discovery, and the joy of shared experiences. And who knows? It might just inspire your guests to embark on their own culinary and mixological adventures.

REGIONAL SPECIALTIES: A LIQUID TOUR OF AMERICA

As we traversed the vast and varied landscape of America in our trusty Priscilla, we found ourselves not just on a physical journey, but on a flavorful odyssey through the country's diverse cocktail culture. Each region we visited had its own unique spirits, ingredients, and drinking traditions, all of which inspired us to create cocktails that captured the essence of place. In this section, we'll take you on a liquid tour of America, sharing the regional specialties we discovered and the drinks they inspired us to create.

The Northeast: A Taste of History

The Northeast, with its rich colonial history and long tradition of distilling, provided us with a wealth of inspiration for classic and innovative cocktails alike.

1. The Boston Tea Party

Inspired by the famous historical event and the region's love for both tea and rum, we created this twist on a classic rum punch.

Ingredients:

- 2 oz Spiced rum
- 1 oz Strong-brewed black tea, chilled
- 0.5 oz Fresh lemon juice
- 0.5 oz Maple syrup
- 2 dashes Angostura bitters
- Garnish: Lemon wheel and a sprinkle of loose tea leaves

Method: Shake all ingredients with ice. Strain into a rocks glass filled with crushed ice. Garnish with a lemon wheel and a sprinkle of loose tea leaves.

The Story: We crafted this drink after a day exploring the Freedom Trail in Boston. The combination of rum and tea pays homage to the city's revolutionary history, while the maple syrup adds a touch of New England sweetness.

2. The Acadian Fog

This cocktail was inspired by the misty coastlines of Maine and the region's famous wild blue-berries.

Ingredients:

- 2 oz Gin
- 1 oz Fresh lemon juice
- 0.75 oz Blueberry syrup
- 0.5 oz Egg white
- 2 dashes Lavender bitters
- Garnish: Fresh blueberries and a sprig of lavender

Method: Dry shake all ingredients, then shake again with ice. Double strain into a chilled coupe glass. Garnish with fresh blueberries and a sprig of lavender.

The Story: We created this drink on a foggy morning in Acadia National Park. The gin represents the brisk sea air, while the blueberry and lavender evoke the park's natural beauty.

The South: Southern Charm in a Glass

The South's warm hospitality and rich culinary traditions inspired us to create cocktails that were both comforting and sophisticated.

3. The Midnight in Georgia

A peachy twist on a classic Old Fashioned, this cocktail captures the essence of Georgia's famous fruit.

Ingredients:

- 2 oz Bourbon
- 0.5 oz Peach liqueur
- 1 tsp Brown sugar
- 2 dashes Peach bitters
- Garnish: Grilled peach slice and a mint sprig

Method: In an old-fashioned glass, muddle the brown sugar with a few drops of water. Add bourbon, peach liqueur, and bitters. Stir with ice. Garnish with a grilled peach slice and a mint sprig.

The Story: This cocktail was born on a warm evening in Savannah, where the scent of ripe peaches and the sound of jazz filled the air. The grilled peach garnish adds a touch of Southern barbecue tradition.

4. The Bayou Zydeco

A spicy, herbaceous cocktail that captures the vibrant spirit of New Orleans.

Ingredients:

- 2 oz Rye whiskey
- 0.75 oz Herbsaint
- 0.5 oz Cynar

- 0.25 oz Simple syrup
- 2 dashes Peychaud's bitters
- Garnish: Lemon twist and a sprig of fresh thyme

Method: Stir all ingredients with ice. Strain into a chilled coupe glass. Express the oils from the lemon twist over the drink and garnish with the twist and a sprig of fresh thyme.

The Story: We crafted this cocktail after a night of dancing to zydeco music in the French Quarter. The combination of rye and Herbsaint is a nod to the Sazerac, while the Cynar adds a complex, bitter note that balances the drink's sweetness.

The Midwest: Heartland in a Glass

The Midwest's reputation for friendliness and its rich agricultural heritage inspired cocktails that were straightforward yet full of character.

5. The Prairie Sky

This cocktail captures the vast openness of the Midwestern plains and the region's famous wheat fields.

Ingredients:

- 2 oz Wheat vodka
- 0.75 oz St. Germain elderflower liqueur
- 0.5 oz Fresh lemon juice

- 0.25 oz Blue Curaçao
- Garnish: Wheat stalk or a long blade of grass

Method: Shake all ingredients with ice. Strain into a chilled martini glass. Garnish with a wheat stalk or a long blade of grass.

The Story: We created this drink while watching a stunning sunset over the Kansas prairies. The blue curaçao gives the cocktail a sky-blue hue, while the wheat vodka and elderflower liqueur evoke the scents of the surrounding fields.

6. The Chicago Typewriter

A bold, spirited cocktail that pays homage to Chicago's Prohibition-era history.

Ingredients:

- 1.5 oz Bourbon
- 0.75 oz Sweet vermouth
- 0.5 oz Fernet-Branca
- 0.25 oz Luxardo maraschino liqueur
- Garnish: Brandied cherry and an orange twist

Method: Stir all ingredients with ice. Strain into a chilled coupe glass. Garnish with a brandied cherry and an orange twist.

The Story: This cocktail was inspired by a visit to a speakeasy-style bar in Chicago. The name references the Thompson submachine gun, popular among gangsters in the 1920s, while the complex flavor profile mirrors the city's layered history.

The Southwest: Desert Heat in a Glass

The Southwest's arid landscapes and fiery cuisines led us to create cocktails that were both refreshing and packed with bold flavors.

7. The Sonoran Sunset

This vibrant cocktail captures the stunning colors of a desert sunset.

Ingredients:

- 1.5 oz Mezcal
- 1 oz Fresh lime juice
- 0.75 oz Prickly pear syrup
- 0.5 oz Ancho Reyes chile liqueur
- Garnish: Half-rim of chili salt and a dehydrated lime wheel

Method: Shake all ingredients with ice. Strain into a rocks glass with a half-rim of chili salt, filled with fresh ice. Garnish with a dehydrated lime wheel.

The Story: We crafted this cocktail after a day exploring the Sonoran Desert. The mezcal provides a smoky base, while the prickly pear syrup mimics the desert's unexpected bursts of color. The chili liqueur and salt rim add a spicy kick reminiscent of the region's cuisine.

8. The Turquoise Trail

Named after the scenic road between Albuquerque and Santa Fe, this cocktail blends Native American and Spanish influences.

Ingredients:

- 2 oz Silver tequila
- 0.75 oz Blue Curaçao
- 0.5 oz Fresh lime juice
- 0.5 oz Piñon syrup
- 2 dashes Orange bitters
- Garnish: Piñon nuts and a turquoise-colored sugar rim

Method: Rim a rocks glass with turquoise-colored sugar. Shake all ingredients with ice. Strain into the prepared glass filled with fresh ice. Garnish with a sprinkle of piñon nuts.

The Story: This cocktail was inspired by the beautiful blue sky and the piñon pines we encountered along the Turquoise Trail. The blue curaçao gives the drink its striking color, while the piñon syrup adds a unique, nutty flavor that's distinctly Southwestern.

The West Coast: Innovation in a Glass

The West Coast's reputation for innovation and its abundance of fresh produce inspired us to create cocktails that pushed the boundaries of traditional mixology.

9. The Silicon Valley Spritz

A tech-inspired twist on the classic spritz, this cocktail captures the innovative spirit of Silicon Valley.

Ingredients:

- 1.5 oz Gin
- 1 oz Aperol
- 0.5 oz Fresh lemon juice
- 0.25 oz Lavender-infused honey syrup
- 2 oz Sparkling wine
- Garnish: Edible flowers and a pipette filled with butterfly pea flower tea

Method: Shake gin, Aperol, lemon juice, and lavender honey syrup with ice. Strain into a wine glass filled with ice. Top with sparkling wine. Garnish with edible flowers and a pipette filled with butterfly pea flower tea.

The Story: We created this cocktail after visiting several tech campuses in the Bay Area. The interactive element of adding the butterfly pea flower tea (which changes the drink's color) represents the transformative nature of technology.

10. The Pacific Rim

This cocktail blends flavors from various Pacific Rim cultures, reflecting the diverse influences on West Coast cuisine.

Ingredients:

- 1.5 oz Japanese whisky
- 0.5 oz Lychee liqueur
- 0.5 oz Yuzu juice
- 0.25 oz Ginger syrup
- 2 dashes Cardamom bitters
- Garnish: A shiso leaf and a slice of starfruit

Method: Stir all ingredients with ice. Strain into a rocks glass over a large ice cube. Garnish with a shiso leaf and a slice of starfruit.

The Story: Inspired by the fusion cuisines we encountered in San Francisco and Los Angeles, this cocktail brings together Japanese, Chinese, and Southeast Asian flavors in a harmonious blend.

Feature Cocktail: The Lotus Flower Lemonade

This refreshing cocktail was inspired by our visit to the beautiful lotus gardens in Echo Park,

Los Angeles. It captures the serenity of the gardens and the rejuvenating quality of a perfect lemonade on a warm California day.

Ingredients:

- 2 oz Vodka
- 1 oz Fresh lemon juice
- 0.75 oz Lavender syrup
- 2 oz Soda water
- Garnish: Lavender sprig and a floating edible lotus flower petal

Method: Shake vodka, lemon juice, and lavender syrup with ice. Strain into a highball glass filled with fresh ice. Top with soda water. Garnish with a lavender sprig and a floating edible lotus flower petal.

The Story: We crafted this cocktail on a sunny afternoon after spending hours wandering through the lotus gardens. The combination of lavender and lemon creates a floral, refreshing flavor that reminded us of the tranquil beauty of the gardens. The vodka provides a clean base that allows the delicate flavors to shine, while the soda water adds a sparkling effervescence that evokes the sunlight dancing on the surface of the lake.

The floating lotus petal not only serves as a beautiful garnish but also adds a subtle, aromatic element to the drink. As you sip, the gentle fragrance of the lotus mingles with the lavender, creating a multi-sensory experience that transports you to those serene gardens.

This cocktail became our go-to refresher during our time in Southern California, perfect for sipping on warm afternoons or as a welcome drink when we hosted new friends in Priscilla. It embodies the laid-back, nature-loving spirit of Los Angeles, with a touch of elegance that reflects the city's glamorous side.

The Great Lakes: Freshwater Inspiration

The Great Lakes region, with its vast freshwater seas and diverse ecosystems, inspired cocktails that were crisp, clean, and reminiscent of lakeside summers.

11. The Superior Sunset

This cocktail captures the breathtaking sunsets we witnessed over Lake Superior.

Ingredients:

- 2 oz Lake Superior-distilled vodka
- 0.75 oz Fresh lemon juice
- 0.5 oz Maple syrup
- 0.25 oz Crème de Violette
- Garnish: Lemon twist and a wild blueberry skewer

Method: Shake all ingredients with ice. Strain into a chilled coupe glass. Garnish with a lemon twist and a skewer of wild blueberries.

The Story: We created this cocktail after a day of hiking along the shores of Lake Superior. The locally-distilled vodka represents the purity of the lake water, while the crème de violette adds a purple hue reminiscent of the stunning sunsets we witnessed.

12. The Mackinac Bridge

Named after the iconic bridge connecting Michigan's upper and lower peninsulas, this cocktail bridges the gap between sweet and savory.

Ingredients:

- 2 oz Michigan rye whiskey
- 0.5 oz Cherry liqueur
- 0.5 oz Sweet vermouth
- 2 dashes Jerry Thomas Decanter bitters
- Garnish: Brandied cherry and a piece of Michigan fudge on the side

Method: Stir all ingredients with ice. Strain into a rocks glass over a large ice cube. Garnish with a brandied cherry and serve with a piece of Michigan fudge on the side.

The Story: This cocktail was inspired by our drive across the Mackinac Bridge and our visit to

Mackinac Island. The cherry liqueur represents Michigan's famous cherry orchards, while the fudge is a nod to the island's renowned treat.

The Rocky Mountains: Peak Flavor

The majestic Rocky Mountains, with their alpine herbs and crisp mountain air, inspired cocktails that were both invigorating and complex.

13. The Aspen Glow

This cocktail captures the golden light of sunset on snow-capped peaks.

Ingredients:

- 1.5 oz Colorado single malt whiskey
- 0.75 oz Génépy des Alpes
- 0.5 oz Honey syrup
- 0.25 oz Fresh lemon juice
- 2 dashes Pine needle bitters
- Garnish: A spruce tip and a dusting of edible gold flakes

Method: Shake all ingredients with ice. Strain into a chilled coupe glass. Garnish with a spruce tip and a light dusting of edible gold flakes.

The Story: We crafted this cocktail after a day of skiing in Aspen. The génépy, an alpine herbal liqueur, evokes the mountain flora, while the local whiskey provides a warming base. The gold

flakes mimic the beautiful "alpine glow" we witnessed at sunset.

14. The Continental Divide

This bi-colored cocktail represents the division
of watersheds along the Continental Divide.

Ingredients:

- 1 oz Gin
- 1 oz Blue Curaçao
- 1 oz Fresh lemon juice
- 1 oz Crème de Violette
- Garnish: A "divide" of lemon peel down
  the center of the glass

Method: In a shaker with ice, combine gin and
blue curaçao. In another shaker with ice, combine
lemon juice and crème de violette. Strain both
mixtures simultaneously into opposite sides of a
chilled martini glass, creating a split of blue and
violet. Garnish with a long lemon peel "divide"
down the center of the glass.

The Story: Inspired by our drive along the
Continental Divide, this cocktail visually represents the separation of watersheds. The gin-based
blue side represents waters flowing to the Pacific,
while the violet side represents those flowing to
the Atlantic.

Conclusion: A Nation in a Glass

As we reflect on our liquid journey across America, we're struck by the incredible diversity of flavors, traditions, and innovations we encountered. Each cocktail we created is more than just a drink; it's a liquid postcard, capturing a moment, a place, and an experience from our travels.

TRAVEL-INSPIRED MIXOLOGY: BOTTLING YOUR ADVENTURES

Our journey across America in Priscilla taught us that every destination has a unique flavor profile, waiting to be captured in a glass. Travel-inspired mixology is about more than just mixing drinks; it's about distilling the essence of your experiences into liquid form. In this section, we'll share our insights on how to create cocktails based on your own travels and provide tips for improvising with local ingredients.

CREATING COCKTAILS BASED ON YOUR OWN TRAVELS

Transforming your travel memories into cocktails is a creative and rewarding process. Here's a step-by-step guide to help you bottle your adventures:

1. Capture the Essence of Place

Start by reflecting on the destination. What were the dominant sights, smells, and tastes you encountered? Was the landscape lush and tropical, or arid and sparse? Was the culture vibrant and spicy, or refined and subtle? These impressions will form the foundation of your cocktail.

Example: During our time in the Southwest, we were struck by the arid landscape, the intensity of the sun, and the prevalence of smoky, spicy flavors in the cuisine. This led us to create cocktails featuring mezcal (for smokiness), prickly pear (for desert flora), and chili (for heat).

2. Identify Key Flavors

Make a list of flavors that you associate with the destination. These could be from local cuisine, native plants, or even non-edible elements that captured the spirit of the place.

Example: In New England, we noted flavors like apple, maple, cranberry, and a briny seaside essence. These became key components in our New England-inspired cocktails.

3. Research Local Spirits and Ingredients

Every region has its own spirits and unique ingredients. Research what's produced locally in the area you visited. If you can't find these exact products at home, look for similar alternatives.

Example: In Kentucky, we naturally gravitated towards bourbon. But we also discovered that the state produces excellent sorghum syrup, which became a key ingredient in our Kentucky-inspired cocktails.

4. Consider the Weather and Season

The climate of your destination can greatly influence your cocktail creation. Hot, humid places might inspire refreshing, lighter drinks, while cold regions might call for warming, spirit-forward cocktails.

Example: Our time in Miami inspired us to create tall, refreshing cocktails with tropical fruits and plenty of ice, perfect for beating the heat and humidity.

5. Incorporate Cultural Elements

Consider the cultural aspects of your destination. Are there traditional drinks you can put a spin on? Any cultural symbols you can reference in your presentation?

Example: In New Orleans, we were inspired by the city's cocktail history. We created a twist on the Sazerac, incorporating local herbs and serving it in a glass rinsed with herbsaint, a local anise-flavored spirit.

6. Name Your Creation

Give your cocktail a name that evokes your travel experience. It could reference a specific place, event, or feeling from your trip.

Example: Our "Painted Lady Priscilla" cocktail was named after our colorfully painted camper, capturing the spirit of our entire journey.

7. Perfect Your Recipe

Experiment with proportions until you achieve a balance that best represents your travel experience. Don't be afraid to make multiple iterations.

Example: Our "Desert Mirage" cocktail went through several versions before we found the perfect balance of prickly pear, lime, and agave that truly captured the essence of the Southwestern desert.

TIPS FOR IMPROVISING WITH LOCAL INGREDIENTS

One of the joys of travel-inspired mixology is working with local, sometimes unfamiliar ingredients. Here are some tips for improvising on the road:

1. Visit Local Markets

Farmers' markets and local grocers are treasure troves of regional ingredients. Don't be afraid to ask vendors about unfamiliar items and how they're typically used.

Tip: We discovered a wealth of unique citrus varieties at a California farmers' market, which inspired several of our West Coast cocktails.

2. Forage Responsibly

If you're in a natural area, consider foraging

for cocktail ingredients. Always ensure you have permission and know how to identify plants safely.

Tip: In the Pacific Northwest, we (carefully and with permission) foraged for wild berries and pine tips, which added unique flavors to our cocktails.

3. Adapt Familiar Recipes

Start with a classic cocktail recipe and substitute local ingredients. This can lead to exciting new flavor combinations.

Tip: In Maine, we created a "Blueberry Mojito" by substituting local wild blueberries for the traditional mint.

4. Use Local Preserves and Syrups

If fresh ingredients aren't available, look for locally-made preserves, syrups, or other products that capture regional flavors.

Tip: In Vermont, we used locally-produced maple syrup to create a "Maple Old Fashioned" that perfectly captured the essence of New England autumn.

5. Experiment with Infusions

Infusing spirits with local ingredients is a great way to capture unique flavors. This technique works well when you're staying in one place for a few days.

Tip: In New Mexico, we infused vodka with

green chilies to create a base for a spicy "Sante Fe Martini."

6. Don't Forget About Local Sodas and Mixers

Many regions have their own unique sodas or mixers. These can add a distinctive local touch to your cocktails.

Tip: In the South, we incorporated locally-produced craft root beer into a boozy "Dixie Float."

7. Embrace Unexpected Ingredients

Don't limit yourself to traditional cocktail ingredients. Local spices, teas, or even culinary ingredients can add interesting dimensions to your drinks.

Tip: In Louisiana, we used file powder (a spice used in gumbo) to rim glasses for our "Bayou Martini."

8. Use Local Techniques

Pay attention to local culinary techniques that might translate well to cocktail making.

Tip: In Texas, inspired by the barbecue culture, we experimented with smoking our cocktail ingredients to add depth and complexity.

9. Balance Novelty with Familiarity

While it's exciting to use new ingredients, remember to balance them with more familiar flavors to create approachable drinks.

Tip: When using the intensely floral prickly

pear in our Southwestern cocktails, we balanced it with familiar citrus notes.

10. Document Your Creations

Keep a travel cocktail journal. Note down your recipes, where you found ingredients, and the stories behind your creations.

Tip: Our cocktail journal became not just a recipe book, but a liquid travel diary, full of memories and inspiration.

Conclusion: Your Journey, Your Flavors

Travel-inspired mixology is about more than just creating delicious drinks; it's about capturing memories, exploring cultures, and telling stories through flavor. Each cocktail you create becomes a liquid souvenir, far more personal and evocative than any trinket you could buy in a gift shop.

As you embark on your own travels, we encourage you to approach each destination with a mixologist's eye. Notice the flavors in the local cuisine, the aromas in the air, the colors in the landscape. Let these sensory experiences guide your cocktail creations.

Remember, there's no right or wrong way to create a travel-inspired cocktail. The most important ingredient is your personal experience. Your cocktail might not taste exactly like the place you visited, but if it evokes the memories and emotions of your journey, then you've succeeded.

So, whether you're sipping a frosty coconut concoction on a tropical beach, or warming up with a spiced hot toddy in a mountain cabin, take a moment to really taste your surroundings. And when you return home, don't just unpack your suitcase – unpack your flavor memories and pour them into a glass.

After all, isn't that what the spirit of a Post Modern Gypsy is all about? Finding inspiration in every destination, creating something unique from your experiences, and sharing the flavors of your journey with others.

Here's to the world of flavors waiting to be discovered, mixed, and enjoyed. May your travels be tasty, your cocktails be inspired, and may each sip bring back beautiful memories of adventures past and those yet to come.

THE ART OF MOBILE MIXOLOGY: SHAKING UP THE OPEN ROAD

Our journey across America in Priscilla wasn't just about the destinations; it was about the art of living well on the road. And for us, that meant mastering the craft of mobile mixology. Creating great cocktails in a moving vehicle presents unique challenges, but with the right approach and tools, it's not only possible but incredibly rewarding. In this section, we'll share our insights on crafting exceptional drinks on the go and the essential tools every traveling bartender needs.

CREATING GREAT COCKTAILS ON THE ROAD

Mobile mixology is about more than just making do; it's about embracing the unique opportunities that come with crafting cocktails in ever-changing environments. Here's what we learned about creating great cocktails on the road:

1. Embrace Simplicity

When you're working with limited space and resources, simplicity is key. Focus on cocktails that require few ingredients but pack a flavorful punch.

Tip: We found that classic cocktails like the Old Fashioned or the Daiquiri, which require only a few ingredients, were perfect for our mobile bar. They're easy to make but still impressive.

2. Pre-batch When Possible

Prepare batched cocktails before hitting the road. This saves time and space, and ensures you always have a delicious drink ready to go.

Example: Before a long drive through the desert, we pre-batched a large quantity of Negronis. At the end of a hot day, we simply had to pour over ice and garnish for an instant, refreshing cocktail.

3. Use Local, Seasonal Ingredients

Take advantage of the changing landscapes by incorporating local, seasonal ingredients into your cocktails. This not only ensures freshness but also creates a unique drink that captures the essence of your current location.

Tip: We made it a habit to stop at local farmers' markets or roadside stands to pick up fresh fruits, herbs, and local specialties to use in our cocktails.

4. Adapt to Your Environment

Let your surroundings inspire your creations. If you're in a hot climate, focus on refreshing, cooling drinks. In colder areas, opt for warming, spirit-forward cocktails.

Example: While traveling through the Southwest, we created a series of refreshing agave-based cocktails that were perfect for beating the heat. In contrast, our time in the Rocky Mountains inspired us to craft rich, warming whiskey cocktails.

5. Master the Art of Improvisation

Be prepared to think on your feet and get creative with substitutions. Sometimes, you won't have access to your usual ingredients, so learning to improvise is crucial.

Tip: We often used honey as a substitute for simple syrup, and lemon juice in place of lime when supplies were low. These small adjustments can lead to delightful new flavor combinations.

6. Prioritize Proper Storage

Proper storage of ingredients is crucial when you're on the move. Invest in good quality, airtight containers to keep your ingredients fresh and prevent spills.

Example: We used a combination of mason jars for syrups and infusions, and small boston round bottles for bitters and other liquid ingredients. These were secure, space-efficient, and helped keep our mobile bar organized.

7. Learn to Garnish with What's Available

Garnishes can elevate a simple cocktail, but traditional garnishes aren't always available on the road. Learn to use what's around you creatively.

Tip: We often used wildflowers, interesting

leaves, or even small souvenirs as unique garnishes that added a sense of place to our cocktails.

8. Perfect Your Outdoor Setup

Creating a comfortable and functional outdoor bar setup is key to enjoying your mobile mixology experience. Consider factors like wind, sunlight, and available flat surfaces when setting up.

Example: We created a fold-out bar that attached to Priscilla's side, providing a stable surface for mixing drinks. We also had a pop-up canopy for shade and wind protection.

9. Practice Sustainable Mixology

Being on the road makes you acutely aware of your resource consumption. Practice sustainable mixology by minimizing waste, using reusable tools, and respecting the environments you visit.

Tip: We composted our organic waste when possible, used metal straws, and always made sure to leave our mixing spots cleaner than we found them.

10. Document Your Creations

Keep a journal of your mobile mixology adventures. Document your recipes, note where you created them, and what inspired each drink. This becomes a wonderful souvenir of your journey.

Example: Our cocktail journal became a cherished record of our trip, full of recipes, pressed flowers, and notes about the places and people that inspired each creation.

ESSENTIAL TOOLS FOR THE TRAVELING BARTENDER

A well-equipped mobile bar is the key to successful cocktail creation on the road. Here are the essential tools we found indispensable during our journey:

1. Versatile Mixing Glass

A durable, multipurpose mixing glass is crucial. We recommend a sturdy pint glass or a stainless steel shaker tin, which can be used for stirring, shaking, and even as a drinking glass in a pinch.

Tip: We found a stainless steel shaker tin to be incredibly versatile and virtually indestructible - perfect for life on the road.

2. Compact Bar Tool Set

Invest in a compact bar tool set that includes a jigger, bar spoon, muddler, and strainer. Look for sets designed for travel, which often nest together to save space.

Example: We used a cocktail kit designed for camping, which included all the essential tools in a compact, zippered case.

3. Folding Knife and Cutting Board

A good quality folding knife and a small cutting board are essential for preparing fresh garnishes and cutting fruit.

Tip: We found a foldable cutting board that doubled as a serving board, saving space and adding versatility to our kit.

4. Portable Ice Maker or Insulated Cooler

Good ice is crucial for great cocktails. A portable ice maker is ideal if you have the space and power. Alternatively, a high-quality insulated cooler can keep ice for days.

Example: We invested in a small, countertop ice maker that plugged into Priscilla's power supply. On days when we were off-grid, we relied on our insulated cooler.

5. Reusable Water Bottles and Containers

A selection of reusable bottles and containers in various sizes is essential for storing syrups, juices, and pre-batched cocktails.

Tip: We used a combination of mason jars, squeeze bottles, and vacuum-insulated containers to keep our ingredients fresh and organized.

6. Lightweight, Durable Glassware

Proper glassware can elevate the cocktail experience, but traditional glasses aren't practical on the road. Look for lightweight, durable alternatives.

Example: We loved our set of stainless steel "glasses" in various styles - they were unbreakable, kept drinks cold, and still looked elegant.

7. Citrus Press

Fresh citrus juice is a cornerstone of many cocktails. A good quality, handheld citrus press is a must-have tool.

Tip: We found a press that worked for both limes and lemons, saving space in our kit.

8. Cocktail Sieve

A fine-mesh cocktail sieve is crucial for straining out small ice chips and ensuring silky-smooth cocktails.

Example: We used a collapsible cocktail sieve that folded flat for easy storage.

9. Reusable Straws and Picks

Eco-friendly, reusable straws and cocktail picks are essential for both practical and environmental reasons.

Tip: We carried a set of metal straws in various

sizes, along with a cleaning brush. For picks, we got creative and often used small twigs or herbs from our surroundings.

10. Portable Power Bank

If you're using any electronic tools (like a rechargeable frother or a portable ice maker), a power bank can be a lifesaver.

Example: Our high-capacity power bank allowed us to run our portable ice maker even when we were camping off-grid.

11. Spill-Proof Travel Bottles

For transporting spirits, invest in spill-proof travel bottles designed for liquids. These prevent leaks and are often more space-efficient than full-sized bottles.

Tip: We used a set of leak-proof, silicone travel bottles for our most-used spirits. They were durable, squishable (great for packing), and never leaked.

12. Multi-Purpose Lighter

A good quality, wind-resistant lighter is useful not just for lighting campfires, but also for flame-related cocktail techniques like expressing citrus oils or lighting aromatic garnishes.

Example: Our refillable butane torch lighter was perfect for creating smoky garnishes and caramelizing sugar for our "Campfire Old Fashioned."

Conclusion: The World is Your Bar

Mastering the art of mobile mixology opens up a world of possibilities. It allows you to create exceptional drinking experiences anywhere, turning each new location into a unique bar with its own special ambiance. Whether you're mixing drinks at a scenic overlook, a beachside campsite, or in the cozy confines of your mobile home, the ability to craft great cocktails on the road adds an extra layer of enjoyment to your travels.

Remember, mobile mixology is about more than just the drinks - it's about the experience. It's about clinking glasses under a star-filled sky, sharing stories around a campfire, or toasting to a breathtaking sunset. It's about capturing the spirit of your journey in a glass and sharing it with fellow travelers and new friends.

As you embark on your own mobile mixology adventures, embrace the challenges and limitations as opportunities for creativity. Let the changing landscapes inspire your creations, and don't be afraid to experiment with local ingredients and flavors. With practice, you'll find that your mobile bar can produce drinks that rival those of any stationary establishment - with the added bonus of ever-changing, spectacular views.

So pack your shaker, stock your mobile bar, and hit the road. Remember, in the world of a Post

Modern Gypsy, every destination is a potential speakeasy, every sunset a cocktail hour, and every new flavor a souvenir of your journey.

COCKTAIL STORIES: LIQUID MEMORIES OF THE JOURNEY

Throughout our journey across America in Priscilla, we found that every cocktail we created had a story to tell. These weren't just drinks; they were liquid memories, each sip a reminder of a place we'd been, a person we'd met, or an experience we'd shared. In this section, we'll share some of our favorite cocktail stories from the road, complete with recipes so you can taste a bit of our journey for yourself.

The Tornado Chaser

Our journey through Kansas took an unexpected turn when we found ourselves outrunning a tornado. The adrenaline rush of that experience inspired this bold, spicy cocktail that leaves you feeling warm and alive.

Recipe: Tornado Chaser

- 2 oz Kansas whiskey
- 4 oz Ginger beer
- 0.5 oz Fresh lime juice
- 2 dashes Angostura bitters
- Garnish: Candied ginger

Method: Build in a copper mug or highball glass filled with ice. Stir gently to combine. Garnish with a piece of candied ginger.

The spicy kick of ginger beer in this drink mimics the adrenaline rush we felt as we sped down the highway, watching the storm in our rearview mirror. The local Kansas whiskey grounds the drink in a sense of place, while the lime adds a bright note that reminds us of the flash of lightning we saw. Each sip of this cocktail takes us back to that heart-pounding moment when nature reminded us of its awesome power.

The Desert Mirage

During our time in the Southwestern deserts, we were captivated by the shimmering heat mirages on the horizon. This refreshing cocktail captures the essence of those illusory oases.

Recipe: Desert Mirage

- 2 oz Prickly pear vodka

- 1 oz Fresh lime juice
- 0.75 oz Agave nectar
- Soda water
- Garnish: Dehydrated lime wheel

Method: Shake vodka, lime juice, and agave nectar with ice. Strain into a collins glass filled with ice. Top with soda water. Garnish with a dehydrated lime wheel.

The prickly pear vodka, infused with the fruit of desert cacti, represents the unexpected bursts of life we encountered in the arid landscape. The lime and agave provide a tart sweetness reminiscent of the resilient plants that thrive in harsh conditions. The soda water adds a refreshing fizz that mimics the shimmering mirages we saw dancing on the distant horizon.

The Painted Lady Priscilla

As Priscilla transformed from a simple camper into a rolling work of art, we felt inspired to create a cocktail that captured her vibrant spirit and the joy of creative expression.

Recipe: Painted Lady Priscilla

- 1.5 oz Pink gin
- 0.5 oz Elderflower liqueur
- 1 oz Fresh grapefruit juice
- Prosecco float

- Edible paint swirl (made with flavored syrups and edible glitter)

Method: Shake gin, elderflower liqueur, and grapefruit juice with ice. Strain into a champagne flute. Top with Prosecco. Create a swirl of edible paint on the surface using flavored syrups mixed with edible glitter.

This cocktail is a liquid tribute to Priscilla's artistic transformation. The pink gin represents her colorful exterior, while the elderflower liqueur adds a touch of sophistication. The grapefruit juice provides a tart note that reminds us of the challenges we faced and overcame on our journey. The Prosecco float and edible paint swirl celebrate the joy and creativity that defined our travels.

Feature: Maw Maw's French Coconut Pie

One of the most poignant memories from our journey was reminiscing about the author's grandmother, Maw Maw, and her beloved French coconut pie. This cocktail is a liquid homage to those sweet memories and the comfort of familial traditions.

Recipe: Maw Maw's French Coconut Pie

- 1.5 oz Coconut rum
- 1 oz Vanilla vodka
- 1 oz Cream of coconut

- 1 oz Pineapple juice
- Garnish: Toasted coconut rim and a sprinkle of nutmeg

Method: Rim a cocktail glass with toasted coconut. Shake all ingredients with ice. Strain into the prepared glass. Sprinkle a dash of freshly grated nutmeg on top.

This cocktail captures the essence of Maw Maw's French coconut pie in liquid form. The coconut rum and cream of coconut provide the rich, tropical base that was the hallmark of her pie. The vanilla vodka adds a sweet, aromatic note reminiscent of the pie's delicate custard, while the pineapple juice brings a touch of acidity to balance the sweetness, much like the perfectly balanced flavors in Maw Maw's baking.

The toasted coconut rim adds a textural element that recalls the pie's crisp crust, and the sprinkle of nutmeg on top is a nod to the warm spices that made Maw Maw's pie so special. Each sip of this cocktail is like taking a bite of that beloved dessert, evoking warm memories of family gatherings and the comfort of home-cooked treats.

As we enjoyed this cocktail on quiet evenings in Priscilla, it served as a reminder of the roots that grounded us even as we embarked on new adventures. It became a liquid connection to home, a way to carry the warmth of family memories with us wherever the road led.

Conclusion: Bottled Memories

These cocktails, and the stories behind them, represent just a small sample of the liquid memories we created on our journey. Each one is a testament to the power of mixology to capture moments, preserve experiences, and tell stories.

As you craft these drinks, we invite you to not just taste the flavors, but to imagine the experiences that inspired them. Picture the vast Kansas sky darkening with an oncoming storm, feel the harsh yet beautiful desolation of the Southwestern desert, visualize Priscilla's transformation into a vibrant work of art, and let yourself be enveloped in the warm, comforting memories of family traditions.

These cocktails are more than just recipes; they're invitations to join us on our journey, to share in our experiences, and perhaps to inspire you to create your own liquid memories. So raise a glass, take a sip, and let these cocktail stories transport you to the open road, where every turn brings a new adventure and every stop is an opportunity to create a new flavor-filled memory.

GLOSSARY

A

Aperitif: A drink served before a meal to stimulate the appetite.

Aromatic Bitters: Concentrated flavoring agents used in small quantities to add complexity to cocktails.

B

Batching: The process of pre-mixing cocktail ingredients in large quantities for later use.

Bitters: Alcoholic preparations flavored with botanical matter, used to add complexity to cocktails.

C

Cocktail: A mixed drink typically made with a distilled liquor as its base ingredient.

Craft Distillery: A small, often independently-owned distillery that produces spirits in small batches.

D

Dry Shake: Shaking cocktail ingredients without ice, often used when a recipe includes egg whites.

E

Edible Paint: A mixture of food coloring and edible ingredients used to create decorative effects on cocktails.

F

Farm-to-Glass: A mixology approach that emphasizes using fresh, locally-sourced ingredients in cocktails.

Flame: A technique used in cocktail preparation where a citrus peel is ignited to release aromatic oils.

G

Garnish: An ornamental addition to a cocktail that complements its flavors or appearance.

I

Infusion: The process of steeping flavoring ingredients in a spirit to impart new flavors.

J

Jigger: A bartending tool used to accurately measure liquid ingredients.

L

Layering: A technique used to create visually striking cocktails by carefully pouring ingredients of different densities.

M

Mobile Mixology: The art of creating cocktails while traveling or in non-traditional settings.

Mocktail: A non-alcoholic cocktail designed to mimic the flavors and complexity of traditional cocktails.

Muddler: A tool used to crush fruits, herbs, or sugar in the bottom of a glass to release flavors.

P

Pre-batching: Preparing cocktails in large quantities in advance for easy serving later.

R

Regional Specialty: A drink that is closely associated with a particular geographic area, often using local ingredients or techniques.

S

Shake: To vigorously mix cocktail ingredients with ice in a shaker.

Stir: To mix cocktail ingredients by gently rotating a bar spoon in a mixing glass.

Strain: To pour a mixed drink through a strainer to remove ice or solid ingredients.

Sustainable Mixology: An approach to cocktail making that emphasizes reducing waste and using eco-friendly practices.

T

Travel-Inspired Cocktail: A drink created to evoke memories or capture the essence of a specific travel experience.

Z

Zero-Waste Cocktail: A cocktail designed to minimize or eliminate waste by using all parts of ingredients and avoiding single-use items.

www.ingramcontent.com/pod-product-compliance
Lightning Source LLC
Chambersburg PA
CBHW040942110726
48006CB00007B/1231